# ROLLING INTO ACTION

*By the same Author*

"OVER THE TOP" in the anthology, *"The Best One-Act Plays of 1934"*, selected by J. W. MARRIOTT. Performed by Research Dept., the General Electric Company.

"THE BELLY OF HELL"—3-act play dealing with tank warfare, read at Little Theatre, London.

"THE CLOCK STRIKES TEN" in *"The Best One-Act Plays of 1935."* Performed by NEILSON-TERRY, Guild of Dramatic Art, Rudolf Steiner Hall.

"ROLLING INTO ACTION"

# ROLLING INTO ACTION

## MEMOIRS OF A TANK CORPS SECTION COMMANDER

### CAPTAIN D. E. HICKEY

WITH A PREFACE BY
MAJOR-GENERAL J. F. C. FULLER
C.B., C.B.E., D.S.O.

**The Naval & Military Press Ltd**

Reproduced by kind permission of the Central Library,
Royal Military Academy, Sandhurst

Published by
## The Naval & Military Press Ltd
Unit 10, Ridgewood Industrial Park,
Uckfield, East Sussex,
TN22 5QE England
Tel: +44 (0) 1825 749494
Fax: +44 (0) 1825 765701
**www.naval-military-press.com**
**www.military-genealogy.com**
© The Naval & Military Press Ltd 2007

# The Naval & Military Press ...

...offer specialist books for the serious student of
conflict. The range of titles stocked covers the whole spectrum
of military history with titles on uniforms, battles, official
histories, specialist works containing Medal Rolls and
Casualties Lists, and numismatic titles for medal collectors and
researchers.

The innovative approach they have to military bookselling and
their commitment to publishing have made them Britain's
leading independent military bookseller.

*In reprinting in facsimile from the original, any imperfections are inevitably reproduced
and the quality may fall short of modern type and cartographic standards.*

Printed and bound by Antony Rowe Ltd, Eastbourne

To

the Memory of

MY FATHER AND MOTHER AND TO MY WIFE

without the help of any one of whom,
the writing of this book would
have been impossible.

" . . . *Ye who come after them forget not their sacrifice;* *claim as your heritage a portion of their spirit, and in* *peace or in war take up their sword of service; so shall* *the living and the dead be for all time bound in one* *fellowship.*"

HAILEYBURY WAR MEMORIAL.

"*Study the past if you would divine the future.*"

CONFUCIUS.

# PREFACE

*R*OLLING *into Action* might equally well have been called *Rolling into History*; for it was a new form of fighting which the tanks established during the last twenty-six months of the World War. Crude and cumbersome though they then were, I for one feel that the more we know of their history, especially from the point of view of those who blazed the trail, the better; because, whilst their organization and strategy lie permanently embedded in official records, how they were fought and what it meant to fight them will die with those who manned them unless their experiences are set down in print.

It is for this reason that I welcome this book, a personal record of one of those many gallant tank commanders without whose courage and endurance the tanks themselves would have been no more than soulless things of iron; for be it remembered that, however perfect is a weapon of war, the limiting factor in its use is always man.

Further, I welcome this book at the present moment, because rearmament stares us in the face, and it is a reminder of how we should rearm our land forces. How machinery excels muscle, and how as machinery is perfected must the soldier's intelligence and quickness of mind keep pace with the machine. To exchange old weapons

for new is not enough, for rearmament carries with
it an exchange of ideas, of new for old and of a
discipline of mind for a discipline of body. These
things can be gleaned from this book.

.          .          .          .          .

A word about the author may interest the
reader. Though not a professional soldier he
comes from adventurous stock, one of his ancestors
fighting in the Irish Brigade under Marshal Saxe
at Fontenoy, and another being a member of the
Franklin expedition. Born in Buenos Ayres in
1895, he was just twenty when he was commissioned to the Suffolk Regiment in 1915. In
December the following year he was transferred
to the Tank Corps, then called the Heavy Branch
of the Machine-Gun Corps, and served in it until
January 1919. Consequently he was in this Corps
for the greater part of its war life; for tanks first
went into action in September 1916.

His war record is an exceptionally interesting
one. He took part in the dismal Battle of
Passchendaele where tanks were literally hurled
into the mud. At Cambrai his section ran the
gauntlet of the German guns and captured the
village of Fontaine-Notre-Dame, a point of great
tactical importance. When, during this battle, on
1st December, the German counter-attack took
place, he was second-in-command of the nineteen
tanks which drove the enemy out of Gauche Wood,
an achievement mentioned by Sir Douglas Haig in
his dispatches.

When the great German attack was opened in

March 1918, Captain Hickey was once again in the thick of the battle and with his tanks covered the retreat of the 2nd Division. And in August that year, during the great tank Battle of Amiens, he was liaison officer between the tanks and the Australians in the front line, and his section had the honour of heading them in the first tank night attack fought, the Colonel of one of the Australian Battalions being shot dead at his side.

.　　　.　　　.　　　.　　　.

From this very brief summary of his war history, the reader, I think, will judge that this book is going to be a thrilling one. And in this he will not be disappointed. But to myself, who watched all these many battles from the Head-quarters of the Tank Corps, what has interested me most is the personal revelation of the writer; that is the psychological point of view of these memoirs. In war, from the Staff outlook, the least difficulty is to plan and to plot, the greatest—to realize what those who are detailed to set the plan into action will feel. Though war may be ninety per cent a matter of weapons, fighting is ninety per cent a matter of nerves. It is in this respect that this book is so valuable to the military student; for time and again nerves creep into the picture. Also is this fact of great interest to the general reader; for however thrilling may be the account of an action and enthralling the clash of arms, reality will be denied unless the feelings of the fighter clearly reveal themselves. It was that great soldier, Maurice de Saxe, in whose brigade of

Irishmen a Captain Hickey once fought, who said: "The human heart is the starting-point in all matters pertaining to war," and it is because another Captain Hickey has so clearly accentuated this truth that I feel his experiences will not be lost on his readers.

J. F. C. FULLER.

# AUTHOR'S NOTE

MY wife and I had listened to the *Tales of Hazard* on the wireless, and she said to me: "Why not one about the tanks?" I did not seriously think the B.B.C. would entertain any effort of mine; but I sent them a draft talk and it resulted in *The Thrust Towards Cambrai* that I was privileged to give on the 18th November 1932, in celebration of the anniversary of the first great tank battle.

My broadcast was a success, and created such widespread interest that I was tempted to embark upon the writing of a book. *Rolling into Action,* about my experiences and actions with the tanks during the Great War, is the result. I have dwelt on the personal note not because I wished to talk about myself, but because I was told that it was the personal experience which really was most interesting. I hope *Rolling into Action* will show that notwithstanding their helplessness when used under impossible conditions, the tanks and their men proved themselves indispensable in winning the War, for it was the decisive success of the 430 tanks in action on August the 8th, 1918, that settled the fate of the German nation. The German leaders have testified to the "overwhelming efficiency" of the tanks, and that August the 8th was Germany's "Black Day".

Summing up the position, General Von Zwehl, in 1921, said: "It was not the genius of Marshal Foch that defeated us, but 'General Tank.'"

B

Thanks are due to *The Royal Tank Corps Journal* for permission to reproduce the substance of articles.

# CONTENTS

# ROLLING INTO ACTION

# CHAPTER I

## ENGLAND. A SECTION COMMANDER

I

THROUGHOUT my childhood the horror of conscription haunted me, for although the son of British parents, being born in the Argentine Republic I was liable for compulsory military service, to which every citizen of that great country is subjected. While possessing a certain dogged perseverance and pugnacity, I was of a peaceable disposition. Military service had no appeal for me, and I hated the thought of bloodshed. As a conscript in South America one might suddenly find oneself embroiled in a nasty and futile revolution. It was, therefore, with relief that I left that nightmare behind when in 1910 I said good-bye to the Argentine and left for England.

The next four years, at a public school and at the beginnings of a university and professional career, had, I thought, removed me from the sphere of military service and political upheavals. Suddenly in 1914 I found myself a victim of Fate, pitchforked into the greatest war in history. Europe became a cockpit, while the Argentine remained at peace. When hostilities commenced,

23

I was nineteen years of age, and in the unusual position of having dual nationality. By the place of birth I was an Argentine; but by blood, British. I could have avoided fighting by abrogating my British nationality and asserting my right to be recognized as an Argentine neutral. But that went against the grain.

My feeling in those days was that while I was fit to fight for myself, I couldn't let others do it for me. Therefore, early in August, I wanted to join up. My father, however, objected on the grounds that I was too young, saying that I could afford to wait another year, and in the meantime should sit for my Intermediate B.A. at the University of London. To my suggestion that I should enlist at once in the Motor Transport, because I could drive a car and had some mechanical knowledge, he replied: "My son will shoulder a rifle." Aflame with patriotism, my father said that any eligible man who did not enlist would be held in contempt after the War and would be unable to look any decent person in the face. One of his oldest friends was a major in the Hussars, and I imagine it was to this friendship that I owe this display of martial spirit. My mother, on the other hand, who had a practical turn of mind and accurate vision, held the opposite view. Perhaps my father really hoped that the War would end before the year was up and my joining up would be avoided altogether. I was their only surviving child.

As a stop-gap, while studying, I joined the University Officers' Training Corps. We wore uniform for parades. In the early days there was a gibe directed at the O.T.C. It was: "All in khaki is not bold," because, of course, as cadets we were not liable to go abroad. However, if the enemy invaded England we should undoubtedly be called out, so that I considered I was doing useful service, and was not merely playing at soldiers. After a year of this, having got through my examination, I put in for a commission and was gazetted to the Suffolks as a Second Lieutenant. While on a course for junior officers at Cambridge, on my way back from field manœuvres on the Gog Magog Hills in November 1915, I had a serious smash from a motor-cycle. Two dogs, one chasing the other, rushed out through a thick hedge at the side of the road, and cut across my front wheel. I was thrown on my head over the handle-bars. By a miracle I was not run over. A bus returning with officers from the manœuvres, which I had just over-taken when the accident occurred, barely managed to pull up in time. I was picked up insensible and taken in an ambulance to the First Eastern General Military Hospital at Cambridge. My collar-bone was broken, and I was unconscious for sixteen hours owing to bad concussion.

After two months in this hospital and a period of convalescence at my home at Hampstead, a Medical Board passed me fit for Light Duty, and I went back to the Suffolks at Wendover. Later, at another Board, I was given the choice of my dis-charge, or of trying a period of Home Service. I chose the latter. Thus for a year after my accident, which I believe saved me from Gallipoli, I was only fit at the most for duty in England. This year was not altogether wasted, for I followed various courses of instruction. By the time I was again fit for

General Service, I knew a good deal about Musketry and the Lewis Gun, having taken a first-class certificate at the School of Musketry, Hythe, and been through the Machine-Gun School at Grantham. It was while at Grantham that I saw outside a newspaper shop a poster with an illustration of a tank.

Machinery had always fascinated me. The tanks fired my imagination, and I was eager to transfer into them. Many and varied were the harrowing tales of the possible fate of the crew of a tank; but I persisted, because the mechanical side and the novelty appealed to me. My father's objection to the Motor Transport because it was not a fighting service was ruled out here, for the tanks, where there was the same mechanical interest, if not more so, could not be classed as noncombatant. I put in for a transfer, as soon as I was passed fit for General Service. The fact that I had a knowledge of a motor-car engine and chassis (it was only a "Humberette"), and had been through the musketry and Lewis gun courses, proved to be an asset, and my transfer soon came through.

On the 10th of December 1916, three months after the tanks were first used in battle, I arrived at Bovington Camp, Dorset, the newly established quarters of the *Machine-Gun Corps (Heavy Branch)*, which was the official name at that time of the tanks. The development of this new arm of the service was so secret that the words *Heavy Branch* were omitted from the official announcements in the *London Gazette*, and from all except military documents. Bovington was between Bournemouth and Weymouth, but the bleakest spot I had yet been in. The camp, consisting of wooden huts systematically arranged in lines, was set among the moors, and was at least two-and-a-half miles from the nearest railway station, which was at Wool. It was horribly muddy, and altogether struck me as being a very good place in which to keep a secret.

Nobody had been long with the tank battalion to which I was posted. In fact it was in the earliest stages of formation, and I was one of the first officers to report to it. Our "lines" in the camp were still only temporary, and I was quartered in a large wooden hut with nine other officers.

At Christmas I could not get leave, as only ten per cent of the officers were allowed away and there were more deserving cases than mine. About then, fifty new officers arrived, and I was settling down quite comfortably. We had moved into officers' quarters, which consisted of a cubicle to every two officers. In spite of bitterly cold weather and snow, the cubicles were quite cosy, as there was a fire in each. Most of the new arrivals had been commissioned direct to the tanks from Cadet Battalions, and I found myself well up in the scale of seniority among the Second Lieutenants, since my commission dated from 1915. As yet the personnel of a tank battalion was not definitely fixed. The Commanding Officer was from the Coldstream Guards, and the R.S.M. was from the same regiment. Discipline was strict, and we did all the latest drill from the Chelsea Barracks. According to the Colonel, smartness on parade was the essence of discipline, and as smartness could only be obtained by constant drill, we spent all our time at it during the first few weeks, except when we were on Brigade Courses of some class of technical instruction or other. On one occasion I was ordered out to drill a squad while the Colonel was on the parade ground. Having had a good deal of experience in this direction, I barked out my orders with precision. The Colonel came up to me. He was evidently pleased, and told me if I continued like that, I should get promotion.

From the beginning of 1917 our Battalion began to take definite shape. Further officers arrived until there were almost one hundred to the Battalion, which finally consisted of three Companies, each with four Sections. My Company Commander was Captain D. H. Pratt, M.C., of the Royal Irish Fusiliers, and owing to my seniority I was given charge of a Section. The Battalion had no tanks so we had to work without them. My Section was divided into four crews, each consisting of an officer and seven men.

## 2

Now commenced the serious business of becoming a competent tank officer, and learning all there was to know about the job. The amount of knowledge required was considerable, and the standard of efficiency was high.

The training was exceedingly thorough considering that so much had to be squeezed into a few months. A tank officer had to be something of an engineer to understand the workings of the mechanism, and for this purpose he underwent special courses at the Brigade tankodrome, where he was also instructed in driving and unditching.

Then there was the navigation of the tank. To learn this he was taught map-reading and compass work. The latter included the swinging of a tank to set the compass. When a compass was placed inside a tank, the mass of metal deflected the needle from a true reading and this had to be adjusted. The same effect was produced when the quantity of metal was altered by the firing of shells from the tank. Later I had practical experience of this in the Battle of Cambrai. In addition, the ordinary knowledge required by an infantry officer was necessary, such as platoon and company drill; rifle, revolver, and Lewis gun practice; bombing and the use of gas appliances. Artillery was another branch to be studied, for a tank officer had to know the mechanism of, and how to use, the 6-pounder gun. He also had to become proficient in signalling, by lamp, flag and semaphore, and how to handle and use carrier-pigeons. Besides all this, he had to have a thorough knowledge of the tactical handling of a tank.

Bovington Camp was thus really a military university. One attended the various courses of the Brigade Schools in the same way as one attended university lectures, with this difference, that the officers were not only students but lecturers as well, for they had to instruct the men.

The competition for sections warmed up, when promotions started to come through in the *London Gazette*. About the middle of April, I was made a lieutenant, the rank and pay dating back to March the 1st. It was always a vexed question whether seniority or service abroad should have a prior claim. Because of my seniority and as I had been in charge of a section, which at that time was the job of a full lieutenant, I had got my second "pip." While I had not seen service abroad, there was another man, Gibson, who had been in France as a private in the Guards, and had subsequently been commissioned as a second lieutenant in the tanks. He was older than I, and felt that his service abroad should supersede my seniority. I could understand his point of view, and we were good friends. Captain Pratt rightly decided in favour of Gibson, who, therefore, got a section. Consequently, for two months I was a general odd-job man, when not on Brigade courses.

In the middle of June, towards the end of my two months without a section, I was at the tanko-drome, acting as a tank-driving instructor. At one place on the edge of the training ground, there was a patch of what looked like long grass. I did not realize it was marshy ground, and a tank for which I was responsible strayed on to it. The tank sank immediately to a depth of about a foot and a half, and was only pulled out with much difficulty by means of a long steel hawser attached to another tank which stayed on firm ground. This unfortunate episode made a lasting impression upon me as to the necessity of testing ground before taking a tank over it, or of keeping to the beaten track. This tankodrome work was abruptly terminated by my being recalled to the Battalion. I knew that Gibson had met with a serious car smash, when returning from Bournemouth with two or three others, one night some weeks previously. In the darkness they had missed a bend in the road, and the car had crashed into the hedge. Gibson's face had been badly cut, and it seemed as though he might be unfit for further service. A nerve which worked an eyelid had been severed, and would probably leave his eyesight permanently defective. I was not told why I had been recalled, but I guessed it was to resume command of my old section. A section commander was now to hold the rank of captain, so this would mean promotion for me.

During the last week of July, I got seven days' leave. Although there seemed to be no immediate prospect of the Battalion leaving England, it was generally considered that these seven days, which we were all getting in turn, would be the last before going out to France.

On my return to the Battalion, on the 31st July, I found that training was being speeded up, so as to have everyone through his full number of courses. There could be no question that something was afoot. As we learnt later, the 31st July 1917, was the beginning of the third Battle of Ypres.

Battle firing was a thrilling spectacle and for a participant most exciting. Tanks advanced towards targets on the slopes behind the cliffs, and the gunners inside the tanks blazed away at these targets. Really bad shots went out to sea, except on a unique occasion when one went into Lulworth Cove to the consternation of the bathers there.

About this time a Royal Warrant authorized the formation of a new corps of the British Army, to be called the *Tank Corps,* and everyone serving in the *Machine-Gun Corps, Heavy Section,* was transferred to it. We were issued with an embroidered tank badge which was sewn on the right sleeve about four inches from the top.

In another company of the Battalion, there had been great discontent owing to the promotion to the rank of lieutenant of certain junior subalterns, with a view to their being given sections. The senior subalterns who had been passed over formed a delegation and expressed their dissatisfaction to the Colonel. They claimed that owing to foreign service, age or seniority, they had a preferential right to sections. As a result, Pearson, who had been second-in-command of a company, was transferred, promoted Major, and made the new company commander. Spray, a section commander and a "temporary captain," in that company, was promoted as second-in-command to Major Pearson.

Of the other three sections, one went to Grounds (known as "Coffee"), from the Leinsters, who had been in the Second Battle of Ypres; one to Gerrard of the Scottish Horse, who had seen service in Egypt; and the third to Edwards, a South African War veteran, from the Malay States. Spray's section, No. 7, remained without a section commander. On the 2nd August, I was transferred from my old company to Major Pearson's, in order to take command of No. 7 Section, and I was told I could expect my captaincy within the next week or two. My new section had been well trained by Captain Spray, who, of course, considered it to be the best in the company. My transfer meant changing my quarters, and I moved into Spray's cubicle, which I shared with him. He had been a schoolmaster at Manchester, and we got on very well together. My batman, Kydd, at his own request, was transferred to my new company so as to continue as my servant.

On the fifth day after my transfer, there was night driving practice. I was, I felt, regarded as an intruder by the officers of the company, so I tried not to make myself obtrusive in any way. I certainly did not wish anything untoward to happen, so that there might be any cause for resentment against me as a section commander and a newcomer. The course for the night driving was like a pulled out "O" with flattened sides. There was a steep bank about thirty yards long at one end, where I was posted. After doing a right turn, the tanks descended this slowly. All went well until one of Gerrard's tank commanders suddenly lost control of his machine at the top of the bank. The tank dashed down at a terrific pace, sparks flying from its tracks. At the bottom it bounced up and down as a boat does after descending a water-chute. I hurried to the tank, and found the commander unconscious, apparently from shock. The crew were badly shaken, having been thrown about inside. The officer recovered after a few minutes. It was not my fault that the accident had occurred; but it was unfortunate that it should happen just at the place I was supervising.

Next day when Brigade Orders came through, I learned I was a captain. About a fortnight later, there was an announcement in the *London Gazette*:

*REGULAR FORCES. TANK CORPS. Temp. Lt. D. E. Hickey (Sec. Lt., Suff. R., T.F.) to be actg. Capt. while empld. as a Section Comdr. (Aug. 8.)*

C

When an officer was transferred from the Regular Army, or the Territorial Force (as in my case), to Kitchener's Army, he was always "seconded," so that at the termination of the War when Kitchener's Army was dissolved, he could automatically return to his old regiment without loss of seniority.

As a lieutenant in the Tank Corps, I had received 9s. 6d. per day, plus 2s. 6d. field allowance, making a total of 12s. Now as a captain, I would receive 13s. 6d. per day, plus field allowance of 3s., amounting to 16s. 6d., a net rise of 4s. 6d. per day.

## 3

During the first week of August there were many conjectures as to the date we should leave; but of one thing we felt certain, and that was that our destination was France. Rumour had it that our departure would take place between the 15th and 31st of August. Davis, who had an eminent friend at the War Office, said we should not leave before the beginning of September. As the hectic days passed, full of preparation and expectancy, the date narrowed to probably the 19th, then the 21st. On the 19th, we learnt that our postal address after our departure would be: 23 Coy., "H" Battalion, Tank Corps, B.E.F., France.

Actually our departure took place on the 21st of August—a Tuesday. We marched to Wool Station, and entrained early in the afternoon, to cross the water that night. We did not know our port of embarkation until we arrived at Southampton in the evening. I was spared the horror of personal good-byes, for my leave had been in July, and then it was uncertain how soon our departure would be. One always hoped for another leave before the fateful day. The morning of our departure, I received at Bovington a letter from my father, and another from my mother, wishing me good luck.

At Southampton, the Battalion, trained to concert pitch, embarked on the s.s. *Londonderry*.

The eight months at Bovington had been well spent, and had produced a first-class unit, with splendid *esprit de corps*.

On board I found that Major Pratt was the Military C.O. for the crossing, and to my lot had fallen the job of "Ship's Adjutant."

# CHAPTER II

# FRANCE. THE TANKS

## I

THIS responsible position proved to be a rather doubtful honour. While I had been receiving my instructions on deck, all the cabins were seized by other officers, among whom were many who did not belong to the Battalion. I had thought there might be a cabin marked "Ship's Adjutant," where I could install myself in state; but instead I found myself without accommodation. Someone suggested that in view of my official position, I should clear a cabin, and make myself comfortable. It was only a short time before that I had been a junior subaltern, and I felt that I was still too new to the rank of captain to start throwing my weight about like that. If I did, I should be deservedly unpopular. I believe I found an odd empty berth in an otherwise crowded cabin, which I made use of from time to time. But I got no sleep, and spent the greater part of the crossing wandering around.

The ship was packed. It was the Adjutant's duty to see that order was maintained on board. I felt if the ship was torpedoed, I wanted to be on the spot to do my job properly. Though I was rather proud of having been selected for it, I did resent not having a proper office. It was a new sensation to be courted for favour by a superior officer. An Indian Army Colonel complained of his "sparse accommodation," and wanted the cabin to himself. He requested me in my official capacity to turn the other occupants out. I refused. With imprecations upon the "Ship's Adjutant," he consoled himself with a bottle of whisky. Before dressing, next morning, he performed on deck his regular matutinal exercises with Indian clubs, to the amusement and surprise of a group of onlookers.

We had an uneventful crossing, and arrived at Le Havre in the early hours of the morning before dawn had broken. In the midst of the scurry and bustle of disembarkation, a hospital train drew in alongside the quay. The scene was typical of those so frequently depicted by Press artists, because of their emotional effect. There were a good many casualties on the train; but a smile of satisfaction and contentment was on their faces, for were they not bound for Blighty? As I watched them a feeling of envy blotted out all other emotions. They had been through hell—but they *had* come through, and had earned the peace and rest to which they were going. On the other hand, I was going into I knew not what, and I had still to prove my mettle. In the haze of a summer morning, we lined up on the quay and marched to the canvas Rest Camp outside the town. I was dead-beat and immediately stretched myself out to get some rest. I had been innoculated two days previously, and that did not improve matters. I scribbled a brief note home on a postcard, announcing my safe arrival, and initialled it in the top right-hand corner, subconsciously I suppose using the spot where ordinarily I should have stuck the stamp. After I had posted it, I was assailed with doubts as to its delivery, for I came across a regulation stating that letters were to be initialled in the bottom left-hand corner, otherwise they would not be "franked". I felt like Alice in "Through the Looking-Glass," and wondered if everything was going to be topsy-turvy. The postcard, however, was duly received at home.

That night four of us had dinner at a restaurant in the Grande Place. There was a delightful air of novelty about it as our table was on the *pavé* outside. The food, though good, was nothing to shout about, and after wine and coffee we were each ten francs the poorer—in English money, eight shillings.

In many ways it was difficult to realize that we were in France. Men in khaki were thronging the streets. Everywhere notices in English were posted up. The atmosphere of war pervaded the town more than in England, for the trams were under the control of, and driven by, the military. As a background, there was the continual distant booming of the guns, though the town itself was miles away from the actual war zone.

Next morning while the men were playing games and doing physical drill, for the double purpose of giving them something to do and keeping them fit, I had my first experience of censoring letters. At the bottom of a letter from a fellow to his girl, there were a number of crosses to represent kisses, and below them he had written: "These kisses are for you. I hope the Censor will not steal them." Censoring letters was a tedious job. Later, each tank commander did it for the letters of his crew, while I censored only those of my batman and runner.

My French improved rapidly, and the little I did know stood me in good stead. On several occasions I was made spokesman. "In the country of the blind the one-eyed man is King." It was fortunate that the others, in their ignorance, did not know the mistakes I made.

During the next three days that we spent at Le Havre, life was easy and pleasant. We felt that we were all on the threshold of a great adventure. For myself, I was remarkably fit and happy. Inexorable forces had been set in motion, and my fate had passed beyond my control. Deep within me, however, was the conviction that everything would turn out trumps ultimately.

We had disembarked on a Wednesday, and the following Saturday we left the camp and marched to the railway station, where we packed into a train. Then followed a long and tiresome journey with many halts. The report went round after one halt, that the train had stopped to enable the engine-driver and fireman to get out and milk a cow wandering near the line, because they wanted milk for their tea. While we nodded and jolted, the train proceeded leisurely through the night and during the next day, so that it was evening when we arrived at our destination.

This proved to be Blangy-sur-Ternoise, a small French village of the agricultural type. I was lucky to be billeted with one of my tank commanders in the largest house in the place, where we were both quite comfortable. I had the good fortune to have a well-sprung bed, and even the comfort of sleeping between sheets, a luxury which I did not have in the Army in England. My men, on the contrary, were not so lucky. I was furious that they had the worst billet of the lot—a filthy cowshed.

By the time we got our quarters settled it was too late, and the men were too tired to start cleaning the place up. Good fresh straw had been laid on top of the filth, and although the smell was far from sanitary, the men were forced to spend the night there.

Round the edge of the cowshed floor, there were food-troughs, filled with straw in which the men were expected to sleep. During the first night, one of them was awakened by something moving the straw beneath him. He found that a pig had stuck its snout through a hole in the wall, and was trying to eat the straw.

In the morning we gave the place a spring-cleaning, and after that it was all right.

The next two days it rained hard, but the cowshed proved comparatively water-tight, and the men picnicking there kept dry.

We found the French people here most hospitable, and nothing seemed too much trouble for them to do for us.

Everybody around was busy reaping the harvest, and food was more plentiful than in England. Our Company was light-hearted. Life was free and easy compared with the rigid discipline of Bovington Camp. Somehow we did not seem to have time to think about the War. Strangely enough, though I had never been closer to the fighting area,

I had never been so absolutely ignorant of how the war was progressing. We were still in an area which was considerably behind the line. Blangy was one of five villages, lying roughly in a circle, which formed the training and rest area of the Tank Corps. Bermicourt, the headquarters of the Corps, was only three miles away, and five miles beyond, as the crow flies, was St. Pol. The other villages in the area were Erin, the Tank Corps Central Workshops and Stores; Eclimeux, where there was a tankodrome and billets; and Humieres, which, like Blangy, was used solely for billeting purposes.

This small state was enclosed in a pentagon, each side of which, from village to village, was roughly about two miles, and it lay west of St. Pol.

Blangy consisted mainly of cottages with pretty gardens and fruit trees, but the picturesque Hospice St. Berthe, built round a courtyard, was a feature, and part of it was used for billets. During the eleven days we were at Blangy, the Battalion was issued with tanks, motor-cars and motor-cycles from the Stores at Erin. At that time it was the plan that each section commander should have a motor-cycle, and the company commander a motor-car. Accordingly, Major Pearson got a beautiful "Vauxhall" car fresh from the works, and we, section commanders, were each provided with a brand new "Triumph" motor-cycle. Making use of these unexpected gifts, Grounds, Gerrard, and myself, went for a joy-ride to St. Pol, while Edwards, the fourth section commander, supervised the officers and men drawing equipment at Erin. In view of my smash at Cambridge, I

treated my "Triumph" with every consideration;
but Gerrard, who in addition to belonging to the
Scottish Horse, had gained a flying certificate in
the R.F.C., made full use of the turn of speed of
which his machine was capable, and of the long,
straight French roads, with the absence of speed
limit.

### 2

From Blangy the Battalion moved in an easterly
direction thirty miles nearer the front line, up to
Wailly, where we arrived on Wednesday, the 5th
of September. On that night a heavy rainstorm
broke over the camp. The officers were quartered
in wooden huts; but the men were under canvas,
and were almost swamped. After that, however,
the weather was glorious. Although we were still
ten miles from the battle front, we felt we were now
getting close up.

Wailly was a small village of ruins on a road
running north into Arras, three miles away. Before
the Germans had evacuated this area in March, this
village, lying just behind our front line, had been
badly shelled, though not to the extent of wiping
it out. To our inexperienced eyes, the damage
seemed considerable. The ruined church, with its
frescoed walls, in its original state must have been
crude; but now, desolate and war-scarred, it was a
pathetic link with civilization. Verdure abounded.
The trees were beginning to take on their autumn
tints, and the air was heavy with the fragrance of
flowers. What had been the German front line was
badly shelled. Compared with it, our old trenches

A FEMALE TANK TRIMMED FOR ACTION ABOUT TO DESCEND A BANK

were in excellent condition, not having suffered such heavy bombardments. Our artillery had been wonderfully accurate. The French had evidently held this part of the line at some time. Although practically everything had been cleared away, here and there were to be found remains of their equipment. Except for small cemeteries, with little wooden crosses, and lines of piled up chalky earth, where the trenches were, cutting irregularly across the green fields, and villages which had been shattered, there was little to show that only six months before, two great nations had been at grips there. Already the villages were being rebuilt, and their former inhabitants were returning to them.

This old battle-field made a splendid training ground on which to test and manœuvre our new tanks over actual trenches and shell-holes.

At Wailly the companies paraded, trained and messed independently, and as a result I rather lost touch with Davis and my former friends. I began, however, to feel at home with my new companions.

The Company had been issued with twelve tanks, and my Section No. 7, was one of the three fighting sections, to each of which had been allotted four tanks. The fourth section, that of Edwards, was to be used as a Supply Section for the others, not having as yet been equipped with tanks. The Company was over-strength, consisting of the Major, the Second-in-Command, four section commanders and twenty-one subalterns, of whom Kennedy was Reconnaissance Officer and Merrell, Workshops.

Consequently I had five officers under me, one being supernumerary. My senior tank commander was a man of some forty-four years (double my age), who had had varied experience in different parts of the world. He had participated in a revolution in Paraguay; he had prospected for gold in Canada; had been torpedoed by the Germans; had joined up in the ranks under a fictitious name, and as such had seen service in Gallipoli. His identity was revealed in Battalion Orders, while we were in England, and instead of by the name of Lloyd, which was his incognito, he was henceforth to be known as the Hon. Cecil Edwardes. The commander of the carrying section had the same name, without the final "e", and to distinguish them in conversation, one was known as the "Honourable," and the other as the "Dishonourable," without any reflection on the character of either.

The tanks had all been given names, which had been allotted under the direction of the Colonel. Edwardes (the "Honourable") had suggested, and particularly desired, the Spanish name, "Hermosa," meaning "Lovely Girl," knowing the word through his acquaintance with Latin-America. This name, in fact, was allotted to his tank, and he was very proud of it.

At this time the battalions of the Tank Corps were known by letters, and the names of the tanks of each Battalion commenced with the letter by which the Battalion was known. As ours was "H" Battalion, all our tanks commenced with an "H".

The other three tanks in my section were: "Hadrian," "Havoc" and "Huguenot," under the command of Hardy, Hughes and McAllister, respectively. These three tank commanders had been commissioned from Cadet Battalions, and had not had previous service abroad. Hardy, who knew the engine of a motor-cycle inside out, was only just out of his "teens," and was clever at engineering; Hughes, about the same age, had been a medical student; McAllister was a "braw bricht laddie frae Glesgae," and a little older.

Being so near such a town as Arras, with historic as well as war interest, Gerrard and I seized the first opportunity to visit it, and jumped a ride there in a light van, known as a "box-body," on Saturday. We found a very comfortable Officers' Club, well stocked with illustrated papers, where not only tea and dinner could be obtained but also a haircut. After a visit to the barber, we explored the town. The town itself had the deserted air of an English provincial city early on a Sunday morning; only a few people were about. The houses were shuttered, and the shops were closed and padlocked. For a while we gazed out towards the line some three or four miles away. The flash of the guns in rapid succession kept the heavens in continuous illumination. We heard that it was not uncommon for shells to fall on the town towards evening. In spite of it being so close to the line, some of the civilian population had returned and opened up their businesses again. These broken shops had stocks of amazing things—scarcely anything useful, but mostly of the souvenir type—cheap and tawdry. Spying some English books in a shop window, I went in and had a look round. To my surprise, I found *The History of Mr. Polly* and *A Knight on Wheels*, both of which I secured.

Strolling along the street from the Hôtel de Commerce, where we had dinner, we found ourselves in the Market-place, and noticed that a performance of some sort was being given in the Municipal Theatre. In we went, and had seats upstairs. It was a crowded house, and I couldn't help thinking that one shell on the building would scupper the whole lot of us. I waited to see a hole appear in the roof and hear the resulting explosion. Fortunately, however, nothing happened in that line, and we spent a pleasant evening entertained by an Army Troupe. On a later visit to Arras, we heard in the Club a story of the reputed first casualty of the American Army in France. Several American soldiers, rather well oiled, were throwing their weight about in a canteen. One of them said to a Tommy: "Wal, when are you gol-darned British goin' to fight?" "Wot abaht nah?" was the immediate reply as Tommy took a jar of rum from the counter and crashed it down on the American's head.

Our work at Wailly consisted of driving practice both by day and night, and the running-in and testing of our new tanks over the trenches and shell-holes of the disused battle-field. After the first week, we did fourteen hours work a day, getting to know and understand the behaviour of our particular machines, which one day we should drive into battle. How near or how far off that day was, we did not know—we believed that we should be at Wailly three or four weeks. There was a persistent rumour that the War would be over by Christmas. Inwardly I hoped it would come true, for, to be absolutely candid, the more I saw of the War, the less I liked it. It was not that I was afraid, though I hated the thought of perhaps losing my sight or being bayoneted in the stomach. I had the natural desire to cling to life; but strangely enough, I did not dread being killed.

I was a fatalist, and believed that every bullet was invisibly marked with the name of its intended victim. If one was marked for me, I could not avoid it. Fate would decree for the best, if one did one's utmost. I had the feeling that I would come through. In the War one clung to anything which gave one hope and courage. While at Cambridge Hospital, I had studied palmistry. My accident was clearly shown in my Line-Of-Life; but otherwise the Line in both hands was unbroken. From this I derived no small consolation, and it was in part due to this, that I felt assured that I would survive the War. Almost unconsciously I noted the Lines in the palms of those around me, as I chanced to see them. Spray's Line-Of-Life was photographed on my brain. It was broken on both hands at a place which would seem to indicate death at about his age. Needless to say, I kept this to myself.

In the meantime, congenial associates, novel work that was full of interest, a job to hold down, and the joy of the open air, all contributed to my perfect health and happiness. Day in, day out, we worked with the tanks. Hardy's methodical mind devised a plan to enable him to keep an eye on the tools belonging to his tank. Each tool had its own particular place in the tool-trays under the floor-boards, and it could be seen at a glance if any were missing. It was a very necessary precaution, for articles were often "borrowed" by another crew and this borrowing had the habit of becoming a

permanent loan, if the missing object was not at
once traced.

Our training was at times not without incident.

A light railway crossed the training-ground near
the camp. Most of the transport on this line was
done at night to avoid observation from possible
enemy aircraft. On one occasion, when the tanks
were engaged on night manœuvres, an accident
occurred which might have had very serious results.
The noise inside a tank was sufficient to drown
almost any noise outside. Consequently a tank
working near the line was unaware that a train was
climbing the slope, for, of course, there were no
lights. There was a crash as the nose of the tank
cut the train in two. The engine and first trucks
chugged merrily up the incline, ignorant of the
disaster, while the rear half of the train careered
with gathering speed back down the slope. At the
bottom of the slope, there was another crash as the
trucks derailed, mingled with imprecations from
men who had been in them, returning to the line
from leave. Fortunately no one was hurt.

The tanks with which we had been issued were
known as Mark IV's. They were unwieldly monsters, each weighing thirty tons, and having a
maximum speed of only three or four miles an hour.
When closed a tank was pitch black inside, but
could be lit by small electric lights in the angle
where the sides and top met. The sides were fitted
with racks, containing shells and ammunition, and
forward on the left side, next to the officer's seat,
was a built-in tank for drinking-water, while
opposite on the right side was a locker for maps
and sundries. As in a battleship, there was a place

for everything, and everything was so fitted that nothing was dislodged when the tank was in motion. This economy of space was essential, for each tank required a crew of an officer and seven men.

The officer and driver occupied two raised seats in the nose of the tanks, and the rest of the crew was confined to two narrow gangways. These gangways were one foot wide and eight feet long, and ran the whole length of the tank on either side of the engine and machinery. It was impossible to stand upright, for the height of the roof at the gangways was only about five feet. The 100-h.p. petrol engine reached almost to the roof; but there was a small platform behind it, covering the machinery. Over this platform was the starting-handle, which it required four men to turn. Two of the crew were known as gearsmen. One occupied a position at the rear of each gangway where he operated the secondary gears. It required the officer, driver and the two gearsmen to swing the tank when its course was to be altered. One of the gearsmen was understudy to the driver. Each track had its own set of two secondary gears, in addition to neutral, and by manipulating these the tank was steered.

Between the officer and gearsman on one side, and between the driver and other gearsman on the other side, were the gunners, two in each gangway.

There were two types of tanks—Male and Female.

A male tank had slightly more room on account of the projections on either side, where each of the

D

two 6-pounder guns was mounted. The gun-layer and gun-loader of each 6-pounder partly occupied these projections. The projections were called "sponsons."

The female tank had only machine-guns, and each of its four gunners worked one of them.

In both types of tank, the officer had a machine-gun in front.

There were reflectors and sight-holes in the armour-plating through which to peep when the port-holes were closed. In the roof of the cabin in front, there was a hole for a small periscope. But in spite of these, one could see very little of what was going on outside, unless one made use of the port-holes and revolver loop-holes.

A tank, complete with its equipment, was reputed to be worth about £8,000.

It was no easy matter to get in and out of these steel boxes. The doorway was only two feet by four feet. In the male tank one entered in a more or less upright position, for the door was vertical. But the door of the female tank was placed horizontally, so that the only way to get in was to lever oneself in on one's stomach. It was like getting into the witch's oven of Grimm's fairy tale. As I had four tanks under my command, I had plenty of practice, and became skilled in the art of negotiating these holes without too much damage either to myself or my clothes.

I took the precaution of having a second watch and having both fitted with glass-protectors. I found, too, that this repeated getting in and out of tanks made my breeches inclined to rise at the knees, so I got a pair of leather straps for the top of my field boots. These straps, around the leg, below the knee, and attached to the boots, kept the breeches in place.

During these days time flew. I never had a minute on my hands. England seemed very far away—almost as though it belonged to another life. My only reminder of it was the daily letters, newspapers, and cuttings, which I received. Those from home took four days in the post. My father sent me *The Times* regularly, and he wrote to me without fail every day throughout my service with the B.E.F. He still cherished ambitions for my future after the War. My studies to become a chartered accountant, and for an honours degree in modern languages, had been interrupted; but he hoped that when I came home again permanently, I would complete them. With the idea that I might become a Commercial Attaché, he registered my name with the Board of Trade, and underlined all mention in *The Times* of such appointments. I felt it all to be very remote from the present scheme of things.

Our joy in the possession of motor-cycles was short-lived, for there was a redistribution of machines, and the section commanders lost theirs. The majority were sent back to Battalion and Company headquarters for the use of runners.

We had not been at Wailly a week when the rumour went round that tanks were to be scrapped, because they had been such a failure in the Ypres Salient ever since the Third Battle of Ypres had commenced on the 31st July. For my own part, I could not see that such a drastic step was necessary, for after all every branch of the service had its limitations. It was as impossible for the Flying Corps to go up and reconnoitre in a thunderstorm, as it was for tanks to go out and work in a swamp. Within their limits both services could do good work; but exceed their limits and disaster was as inevitable in the one case as in the other.

Our tanks seemed to be intended for work in the Salient; accordingly I did not think it likely that we would do much before the spring. The sodden condition of the ground would not permit, and the War might be over by then. Grounds, who had taken part in the Second Battle of Ypres, talked with first-hand knowledge of conditions in the Salient. One felt that this previous combatant service placed those who had had it in an exclusive caste.

Edwards (the "Dishonourable") would adroitly cap each of Grounds's reminiscences with a reference to his own experience in the South African War. I, who had still to be initiated in actual warfare, felt that I was in the kindergarten stage, while these *vieux braves* had received their remove into the Upper School.

It came as a surprise to learn of the comparatively successful tank action of the 20th September near Inverness Copse, along the Ypres-Menin road, in the Salient; followed on the 26th September by an assault by fifteen tanks, near Zonnebeke village, which, on the other hand, was a failure. We now began to feel certain that we were destined for the Salient in the near future.

It had been instilled into us that a tank commander's duty was to stick to his tank to the end, his whole object being to protect it. If need be he must, like the captain of a ship, perish with it.

Six of my fellow-officers gave me the names and addresses of relatives or sweethearts, to whom I should write in the event of anything happening to them. Four of these fellows had a fiancée or wife. I rather envied them.

My father became greatly alarmed for my safety, when the news of these tank actions reached England, and wrote anxiously asking for news concerning myself, to know if I had been engaged in them, and, if so, how I had fared. I thought that he felt hurt that he had not received a letter from me every day, letting him know that all was well. I reassured him that he need have no fear for my safety as long as he continued to receive one letter per week from me. When possible I would write more often; but I reminded him that working fourteen hours a day, did not leave much time for letter-writing. I promised him that I would write at the week-ends, as I had done up to the present. Any mid-week letters, however, were extra, and should he not receive any, he must not become alarmed. As soon as possible after a battle, I would let him know how I was, and if I were unable to do so, I had arranged that someone else would.

On Sunday night, the 30th September, the "Curios" gave a concert in one of the hangars. A large audience enjoyed it immensely. This performance proved to be the last that the troupe were to give.

Next day, the 1st October, we started to get the tanks ready for a move. Before a male tank could travel on a train, the sponsons had to be unbolted and slid into the interior of the tank. The tanks were drawn up in line and each crew was busy with its own machine. It was one of those warm sunny days which make one feel cheerful in spite of oneself. About noon, the Battalion cooks were preparing the midday meal on the cook-house fire in the open about a hundred yards away. Though no doubt contrary to the regulations, it was the custom to boil water in disused petrol tins. Consequently, when there came unexpectedly the noise of a terrific explosion, I thought that someone had by mistake put a tin full of petrol on the fire. As I looked round in amazement at the cloud of smoke and earth which flew up into the air, taking the men's dinner with it, I was about to express my opinion of the mentality of the bleeding fool who was so careless. Enlightenment followed immediately, however. There was a whisper which quickly became a scream, then another crash, and a cloud of earth and smoke rose from the ground, not from the cook-house this time but a few yards away from it. This left no doubt in our minds that we were being shelled. For the next hour and a half we were treated to similar explosions at five-minute intervals. At the beginning eight shells fell within a hundred yards of me.

After the first shock, the men went about their work as usual. When it was realized, however, that the bombardment was going to continue, we were all ordered to put on our steel helmets, carry our box-respirators in case of gas shells, and take cover. It is wonderful what a sense of security a ditch can afford.

During the whole of those unpleasant ninety minutes, Merrell, the Workshops Officer, carried on with his job on top of one of the tanks.

The first shell did the damage. Davis's cook was struck by a fragment and died on the operating table. My Section cook received concussion and shell-shock from the force of the explosion, and was sent to hospital. There were no other casualties, but part of the light railway was destroyed by the shelling.

This was our first experience of shell-fire. I thought of the irony of Fate. Here we were ten miles behind the line, and the men whom Fate selected as her first victims in the Battalion, were two cooks, who, one would have thought, were comparatively safe in non-combatant jobs.

Remembering how it was only through a friend of mine that my parents had heard of my accident at Cambridge, I resolved then and there to write to the relatives of any of my men who became casualties, to give them what consolation I could. This good intention was not kept, for later on the number and nature of the casualties made mere words seem utterly futile, and I had not the time to carry on the correspondence which each well-meaning letter of mine usually started.

The following morning an unexploded shell was found. It measured thirteen inches across the base, and had evidently been fired from a large German naval gun, mounted on a railway truck.

As a result of this experience, I felt I should be much more comfortable with a concussion pad tucked inside my helmet, and immediately wrote home for one, like one I had seen at Harrods.

One of our last jobs was to decorate the tanks with streaks of paint so as to conceal peep-holes and reflector slits.

On Wednesday, the 3rd October, exactly four weeks after our arrival, we left Wailly, and entrained at Beaumetz for the Ypres Salient.

# CHAPTER III

# THE THIRD BATTLE OF YPRES. POLDERHOEK CHATEAU AND THE LOST PARTY

## I

WHEN tanks had to be moved farther than, say, ten miles, they were transported by train, if possible, to save the wear and tear of the sprockets and rollers, which wore out very quickly.

Each Company moved independently; there was one train to a Company, consisting of one third-class carriage for the officers, horse-boxes for the men, and twelve specially constructed trucks for the tanks.

The entrainment of a company of tanks was a very delicate operation. The twelve trucks were shunted to a ramp, up which the tanks were driven on to the train. The first tank crawled along eleven trucks until it reached the twelfth. As both entraining and detraining were generally done under cover of darkness, it required great patience and skill. One tank badly driven would delay all the others behind it. Each truck was a long, low float, mounted on two four-wheeled bogies. Arrived at its proper truck each tank had to be manœuvred on to two beams placed across the truck between the bogies, so that the weight was evenly distributed on two points, instead of it all being borne at the middle of the truck.

Spray, as second-in-command of the company, had charge of the allocation of officers to the various compartments in the antiquated third-class carriage with its uncomfortably upright, wooden seats, and of the disposal of the men into the horse-boxes marked *Hommes 40, Chevaux-en-long 8.* He took his position very conscientiously, and made the arrangements with great thoroughness, distributing the officers with arithmetical accuracy. Major Pearson critically remarked on the congestion in the compartment, and suggested that a rearrangement might be made, to give greater comfort to the company headquarters staff. Spray, looking at it from the point of view that we were now on Active Service, and well off to be in a train ten miles behind the line, said: "Remember what the poor infantry have to suffer in the trenches." Pearson curtly replied: "Let's forget about them for to-night, and make ourselves comfortable."

Next morning we detrained at Ouderdoom, Belgium.

Immediately on our arrival, I, with other section commanders, was sent forward to find a route for my machines up to a position from which they could be launched into action.

Tanks had already suffered disastrously in the Salient. Every action with them had been a deadly gamble. Nevertheless we were to take part in the final assault on the Passchendaele Ridge, which was to end the Third Battle of Ypres.

Gerrard and I decided that we would do the job together, as we had received similar orders. Major Pearson's "Vauxhall" was placed at our disposal, and took us to Voormezeele, about two miles south of Ypres.

From there we started to walk eastwards the four miles or so towards the British front line and to study a problematic route. Roads, being a standing target, were to be avoided at all costs; besides, if a tank became disabled on a road, it effectually stopped all traffic.

Not fully realizing what we were in for, we chatted cheerfully as we plodded across the green fields out of Voormezeele. We crossed the canal and were pushing our way through a copse, when a sudden discharge of heavy gunfire close at hand, made us jump, and brought home to us the fact that a loud and unexpected noise like that in our ear-drums, was decidedly unpleasant. We wondered uncomfortably where the battery was hidden, and if we were likely to walk into its line of fire. We went cautiously and got away from it.

As we trudged along, the awful nature of the Salient gradually became apparent. Now the copses and fields gave place to a horrid water-logged swamp, and the ground was shell-pocked, boggy clay, with not a blade of grass nor a tree that had not been torn to pieces by shell-fire.

Across Zillebeke Lake on our left, we could see the ruins of Ypres. Shells were whizzing overhead, some—perhaps "duds"—falling with a dull splash into the lake. A main road into Ypres we had just crossed gave proof that the enemy had it well taped, for his shells had blown holes the area of a small house in and along both sides of it. In spite of this a "Holt" tractor was doing a job of work on the road, quite unconcernedly, as though it were in a peaceful countryside.

To add to our discomfort the whole area bristled with our own guns, their squat and long noses poking out of the ground, where they were half-buried for concealment. They were discharging all around us, first here and then there. We never knew where the next detonation would come from and hoped it would not be just at our heels.

For two-and-a-half miles we plodded on across slippery mud, threading our way among the guns, until we came to a spot bearing the rustic name of Valley Cottages. The cottages, if they had ever existed, had been wiped off the face of the earth. At this spot there was a track made of hardwood logs, like railway-sleepers, laid flat, one after the other in endless procession. This "corduroy road" (as it was called) marked the original lane, now completely obliterated by shell-fire. A shell had evidently just crashed at the edge of the track, and the torn ends of the logs were still smouldering, burnt by the explosion. The earth on both sides of the corduroy road was sodden. Here and there at the side of the road were the bodies of pack-mules. They had been taking up shells, and slipping off the greasy track had sunk in the mud. I heard afterwards that it was impossible to release the terrified beasts when they became stuck, and they had to be shot on the spot. It was obvious that tanks could not cross this ground, and even a corduroy road was impossible, for the weight of the tanks would smash it and their tracks would rip it to pieces.

It was a dismal day, and a cold bleak drizzle was falling. As we reached the track the drizzle turned to a steady downpour. The enemy had begun to "strafe" the area, and heavy shells were dropping all around. One disadvantage of the Salient was obvious: in it one received the concentrated bombardment of the enemy guns, firing inwards from two sides of a triangle. We took shelter in a shanty made of rusty sheets of galvanized iron, where we found other tank officers. The overcast sky, the deafening noise and the sense of impending doom, played havoc with our nerves. But whatever our inward feelings were we tried to look unconcerned. It was too much, however, for one fellow. He was sitting on the ground hugging his knees, when suddenly he leaned forward, and burying his face in his hands, burst into strangled sobs. Shortly afterwards he transferred back to the unit from which he had come. At last the bombardment stopped. Gerrard and I started off again, to be able to say that we had at least looked for "lying-up" positions for our tanks. Although, if we found such places, how the machines were to get there we could not imagine.

According to the map, this countryside had once been rich estates of lovely woods and carefully cultivated fields, dotted with prosperous farms and châteaux. It reminded one of a lovely face whose beauty had been totally destroyed by the terrible ravages of smallpox. Now it was scarred and pitted with shell-holes, filled with water and mud.

A mile farther along, past Observatory Ridge,

finding some duckboards which made a rough foot-
path, we left the corduroy track and followed them
to the left towards the Ypres-Menin road. They
were slimy with the rain, and we slipped and
skidded. As we cut through Sanctuary Wood—a
wood only in name, for the trees had been battered
to pieces—the enemy's light artillery started a
barrage there. The few men who were about disappeared into dug-outs, and the neighbourhood
appeared as empty of human beings as a street
swept by a sudden downpour of rain. As we
increased our pace I caught sight of two artillery
officers standing in the doorway of their dug-out
watching us. It crossed my mind that they must
think that we were a couple of inexperienced fools
to behave as we were doing. As we crossed Jack-
daw trench we heard the scream of a shell coming
straight towards us. Gerrard seemed to be gifted
with a sixth sense which enabled him to know
exactly where an approaching shell was going to
drop. He yelled: "Duck!" and we both hurled
ourselves flat in a shell-hole. On my downward
flight I saw a shadowy, egg-shaped thing just about
to strike the earth in front of us. It fell six feet
short, exploded, and the fragments flew over us.
The enemy had chosen for his barrage the path
we had intended following. We changed our
plans hurriedly and ran for it across shell-holes
forward towards the front line. For the moment
that seemed the safest place, because shells were
not falling there.

We struck the Ypres-Menin road at Clapham
Junction. Scrambling up the embankment, we
found some Royal Engineers at work at this par-

ticular spot. We were out of breath, and very glad of the drink of water they gave us in a dixey. After the slimy waste we had just struggled across there was something stable about a main road where men were working. It was at Clapham Junction we saw what had happened to tanks when they had gone off the causeway into the swamp below. They had sunk in the marsh and been knocked out by direct hits from a light gun in a concrete "pill-box" as they had crept too slowly forward. There lay anything up to a dozen tanks—derelicts with huge holes blown in them, and their tracks smashed to pieces. They had met this fate in the advance during the previous eight weeks. The front line had since been moved forward and was about a mile ahead.

It struck me that if the Tank Corps was to be scrapped, putting it to work under impossible conditions, such as these, was a certain way of doing it.

As we returned to Ouderdoom, Gerrard said to me: "What a hope *we've* got!" referring, of course, to our chances in the Salient. With which I entirely agreed.

That evening at a restaurant near Ouderdoom we had a dinner exquisitely cooked and served in the best Parisian fashion. At dinner we heard that tanks had been in action that morning, about a mile to the north of the Ypres-Menin road. The attack had been a success, owing to the perseverance and courage of the section commander, Captain Robertson.

He had to get his tanks across a marshy stream, called the Reutelbeek, at the one available crossing point. His objective was just beyond. The road had been demolished by shell-fire, and the swampy nature of the ground made it necessary to test every step of the way to prevent the tanks being ditched.

Captain Robertson walked in front of his leading tank, prodding the ground with his stick, in spite of machine-gun bullets and heavy shell-fire against the tanks. He must have known that under these conditions his devotion to duty meant sooner or later certain death for him. He believed, however, that the success of the attack depended upon his making sure of the ground over which his tanks were to go. They had crossed the stream, and were approaching their objective, when he was killed by a bullet through the head, while still leading his tanks.

Gerrard and I, after our experience of that day, realized only too well what he had had to contend with, and what a wonderful show he had put up. Robertson, a Haileyburian, by his gallant action, won the first V.C. for the Tank Corps. We felt that he had set a standard which we should find it very difficult to live up to.

2

We expected any moment to get our orders for action, and a day or two later the tanks moved up, under their own power, from Ouderdoom to Voormezeele. It poured with rain the day the journey was made.

We waited; but the attack we anticipated did not come off. Instead of going into action, the tanks were hidden in the hedges and under trees at Elton Point, Voormezeele, with camouflage nets over them.

Under orders, I took two of my section, "Hermosa" and "Huguenot," to a lying-up position just off the Ypres-Menin road, near Birr X-Rd, a spot about two miles behind the line. We had special permission to use the road, and our route took us through Ypres itself. A shiver went down my spine as I saw the devastation of what had once been a fine city. The glory of the Cloth Hall could still be imagined from the magnificence of its ruins. Although there were streets where the houses had not been blown to pieces, most of the buildings had lost their original shape.

As a small boy in Buenos Ayres, I was allowed during holiday-time to visit the "Palacio de Novedades" in Calle Florida, where there was a very realistic model of the earthquake in San Francisco. There was the city intact, then with a convulsive shudder the buildings trembled, staggered drunkenly, and collapsed, leaving just such a scene as met my eyes in this desolate city of Ypres. The road we followed through the town was cobbled. Shells had tried to do their worst to it; but the century-old stones stubbornly resisted the impact in a remarkable degree. Instead of craters, there were only shallow pot-holes. As we passed through the Menin Gate, the famous highway, bordered with derelict tree trunks, stretched long and straight before us.

There seemed to be no immediate prospect of storming the Passchendaele Ridge with our tanks. Any plan for using them as fighting weapons

E

appeared to have been abandoned. In an endeavour to find a job for tanks, my two were being sent forward to be used experimentally as tractors for hauling guns and supply sledges.

Very soon after our arrival at Birr X-Rd we had a chance to show what we could do. A lorry had gone off the road and its wheels became embedded in the mud. It happened to be close to where the tanks were parked. One of them succeeded in pulling the lorry on to the road again. Similarly, a 6-in. howitzer was unditched at Birr X-Rd itself. In each case the tank was able to remain on the road. Later, a 60-pounder was also freed from the mud with the aid of a tank.

Like the other parts of the Salient we had seen, all around was a wilderness of mud, without any natural cover. I expected that any day my tanks at Birr X-Rd would be spotted from the air, and blown to pieces.

I was sent to investigate what could be done about two guns which were half-buried in the mud just west of Maple Copse. I reported that the ground over which the tank would have to go was impassable, and the haulage of these guns was not attempted. In Maple Copse itself shells had torn the sodden earth, disturbing the resting place of several dead. Their legs were sticking up at grotesque angles out of the mud.

I reported also that it was impossible to attempt to shift a gun in Sanctuary Wood; but at Zouave Wood an experiment at gun-haulage was successful.

General Courage, who was in command of our Tank Brigade, paid an early visit accompanied by the Brigade Major, Stephen Foot, to the two tanks at Birr X-Rd. After a conference with our Colonel and our Company Commander, the party turned homewards, following a duckboard track, and so taking a short cut to the Menin road. The path led across the Bellewaarde-beek, which was little more than a ditch filled with water. The duckboards were slippery. I was at almost the end of the procession, and the General was well ahead. Suddenly his foot slipped and he lost his balance. Looking up I saw the distinguished officer with his two legs up in the air, coming down in a sitting position in the mud. His cane flew out of his hand and was rescued by the Brigade Major. I have a mental picture of a red-tabbed staff officer making several unsuccessful attempts to restore the stick to the General, who, floundering in the mud, was more concerned with regaining his feet than recovering his lost cane.

When the tanks were not being used a guard was left in charge. One morning as they were getting out of the tanks a stray shell exploded close by. Two or three of the men were killed by fragments. The poor fellows were buried at night near Voormezeele. Their bodies, each covered with an army blanket, were carried on stretchers. The Sergeant-Major, who was in charge, led the procession as it entered the cemetery. He was obviously feeling the strain. The guns in the Salient boomed. The Padre conducted the simple service as we stood at attention round the common grave. Shells dropped at the outskirts of the enclosure. By the light of a hurricane lantern, which the Sergeant-Major carried, we saw the dimly-outlined forms, as they were laid reverently in the shallow pit. The service ended; we saluted, and went silently away.

Gerrard and I walked back together to the dug-out, which we shared. He was a big man of athletic build, four years older than myself, and extraordinarily sensitive. Dinner was ready when we reached the dug-out; but neither of us felt like eating. The scene we had just witnessed had got on our nerves. At last Gerrard said gruffly: "This is doing us no good. Come on, let's pull ourselves together." Over dinner we deliberately tried to distract our thoughts by talking of the various shows running in the London theatres.

That night feeling certain that I could not sleep I took a stiff dose of rum, hoping that it would act as an opiate. It brought a glow to my body; but instead of dulling my senses, it warmed my imagination to fever heat and kept me awake.

One of Gerrard's tank commanders, Glanville, a courageous and reliable officer, was sent to report on the chances of extricating a battery embedded in the mud about 150 yards from the corduroy track which formed a loop-way for the Menin road south of Hooge. This was half-a-mile nearer the front line than Birr X-Rd. He discussed the proposition with the battery commander. Glanville formed the opinion that the task was impossible and the battery commander agreed. "Nothing can shift these guns," he said. "They have been here for months, through winter and summer, through frost and snow. They are now a fixture, and part and parcel of the Salient." Glanville reported accordingly, and added that a tank working there might easily be seen by the enemy either from an observation balloon or an aeroplane, as the position was exposed. Hearing this, Manning, another tank commander, with sublime self-assurance, volunteered to take a tank up by night and get the battery out under cover of darkness. He was allowed to try. He took (I think) "Hermosa," and hitched it to one of the guns. He gave the order to advance. The tracks spun round, but instead of gripping they dug into the soft earth and the tank sank quickly until it "bellied" in the mud; but the gun had been loosened. Now it was a question of moving not the gun, but the tank. Throughout the night herculean efforts were made to unditch it; but each successive attempt was unavailing. Towards dawn the battery commander began to get excited, because he feared that as soon as the tank was spotted, the enemy would shell them unmercifully. To each exhortation from the battery commander to get the tank away, the tank commander replied optimistically that another few minutes would see him through. Exasperated, the battery commander sent for horses. A team arrived, was hitched to the gun, and plunging and struggling succeeded in pulling it away. Dawn broke. The tank was still stuck fast. The enemy soon observed it, and commenced shelling. Manning was struck in the foot by a splinter, and was carried off on a stretcher. There the tank stayed until later, when with the assistance of another tank and a gang from workshops, it was released.

It infuriated me to see valuable lives and machinery risked in this unimportant work for which tanks were quite unsuitable. When correctly used they would, I felt sure, prove their real worth. It was obvious that tanks could not be satisfactorily employed in the Salient, and it seemed contrary to common sense to persist in such unnecessary waste.

There was a battery of enormous siege-howitzers on the ridge behind Westhoek. These guns were to be brought back to the south-west corner of Zillebeke Lake. I went to see the battery commander, and it was obvious to me, on seeing the guns and the ground, that it was a quite impossible job for tanks. Major Street, the commander, was surprised to hear that tanks were to be used, and thought that the best means of transport was, in pieces, by the light railway which had brought them up. But it was not for us to decide. We exchanged official addresses in case we had to communicate with each other. He glanced at the note I gave him and looked at me. Then he asked reflectively: "Are you by any chance a relation of the Hickey of Argentina?" I replied jokingly: "I am the son of the Hickey of Argentina—the secretary of the Buenos Ayres Great Southern Railway." "I know the name well," he said. "I was out in Buenos Ayres in the Engineers' Department for thirteen years." I was about to leave the dug-out when shells began to crash outside. He refused to let me go, and insisted on my staying to lunch. I made my report when I got back, but heard no more of this futile scheme.

While my two tanks were experimenting in the Salient the men of the Battalion did fatigues, and at Dickebusch helped the Australians to build a plank roadway.

(*Above*) BEET-ROOT FACTORY, FLESQUIÈRES
The orders for the attack and capture of Fontaine-Notre-Dame were
received here
(*Below*) A VICTIM OF THE MUD IN THE YPRES SALIENT

## 3

Since our arrival, Gerrard and I had shared a
dug-out. It consisted of a curved sheet of metal,
about 20 feet long by 6 feet wide, placed on the
ground. Both ends were sand-bagged, and the roof
was similarly strengthened. It would not stop a
direct hit, but it was a protection against splinters.
A narrow trench about two feet deep ran the whole
length of the interior, leaving a shelf on either side.
All the dug-outs in the neighbourhood were made
on the same principle, for the ground oozed water.
The floor of the trench was made of duckboards.
Occasionally after heavy rain, which swept down
through the entrance, the water rose to the level of
our beds. When this happened during the night,
Gerrard, though champion fast swimmer of
Scotland, showed no pleasure at the prospect of
an early dip, and we both waited for our batmen
to bale us out in the morning. One end of our
particular dug-out was in the hedge surrounding
the field, and at this end there was a fireplace
ingeniously constructed from ammunition boxes,
empty shell-cases, and bricks. The other end had
steps leading up to the outside. Gerrard, with the
two batmen, was responsible for the building of the
dug-out, while I was taking my tanks up to Birr
X-Rd, and he never let me forget that he was the
architect of our snug quarters. The left side of the
dug-out was Gerrard's property, and the right side
was mine. We had stretchers for beds, placed on
the shelf on either side of the fireplace. One fellow,
who had been commissioned from a cadet battalion

and had won the D.C.M., slept in the trench of his dug-out, instead of on the shelf at the side. Water oozed up through the ground during the night, and the dampness caused his death from pneumonia.

Within a week I had contracted a cold, which fortunately turned to nothing worse. The weather was terribly wet. The rain came down at the rate of one inch per day. Never before had we been so isolated from civilization. Letters and papers took ten to twelve days to reach us. I had even to ask for pencils and rubber to be sent from home. During the time we were in the Salient we lived a hand-to-mouth existence. Up to now I had refused offers of food from my mother, for the Mess was well provided, and all kinds of little extras could be obtained in the villages round about. Now, however, like a famished schoolboy, I asked for a cake.

In addition to the rain, the weather was bitterly cold. I wrote home for a woollen khaki helmet and knitted gloves. One of the battalion cooks to fortify himself against the cold, tapped the rum-jar. On his way back to his quarters, overcome by the drink, he stumbled, and lay in a stupor where he fell. The intense cold chilled his overheated body and he was found dead in the morning.

Because two of my tanks were up forward, I had to go into the Salient every day. Each time I was seized with nerves, and never went up without feeling that at least one shell would burst close by. Our guns seemed to have an endless supply of ammunition. Although the enemy's reply was meagre in comparison it was bad enough. It did not require a barrage to kill one; a single shell was sufficient, as we had found to our cost.

I got into the habit of having a sort of bet with Fate: if I found a horseshoe pointing the right way I felt I should get back to the dug-out safe and sound. As the Salient was strewn with horseshoes the odds were in my favour.

Just as in London it requires a heavy downpour of rain to clear the streets, in the Salient a heavy bombardment was necessary to make people take cover. Little or no attention was paid to stray shells, and the men carried on with their work.

My father, with natural interest, followed all the movements of tanks reported in the papers, and made guesses as to where I was. I could not give him any names; but as the attention of the general public was focused on the Salient, he correctly assumed that I was there. With youthful bumptiousness, I assured him that I was in a very hot corner, generally considered to be the hottest corner of the British Front. After my request for a concussion pad, he offered to send me a "bodyguard." I replied that it would not be much use against high explosive shell, which was what I had to guard against then, and that it would be too heavy to wear comfortably. I told him that I had been most fortunate—one shell had burst only six feet away!

A girl whom I knew in London, the only daughter of a wealthy Brazilian banker, wrote telling me of the good time she was having. I bore such people a grudge when I thought of the horrors which were happening near me every day. Rather scathingly, I wrote back that I supposed, after all, the sufferings and hardships of the fellows out here were not in vain, if, as one read in the papers, the people in England were still able to have a good time. As a peace-offering she sent me a handsome thermos flask in a leather case, and told me she had joined up as a V.A.D.—hours 6 a.m. to 8 p.m., having signed on for a period of six months.

My father and several of my friends told me in letters of the air-raids on London. The Zeppelin raids were given, I thought, far too much prominence, and it used to irritate me intensely that so much fuss was made about them and reprisals. We were at war, and it was only to be expected that London would be bombed. I had not been in action with the tanks; but I had already had a fair experience of shell-fire. With perhaps pardonable pride, I assured them that the air raids over London might be a great deal worse. Every night squadrons of enemy bombing-planes flew over us at two-hourly intervals, and the shells of long-distance guns screamed as they passed every four to fifteen minutes. Some nights a bomb or a shell would crash in our field, and next morning we would go out to see the damage done. But after the day's work in the Salient we considered our dug-out a haven of peace to which to return to sleep.

One night the enemy was particularly active with bombs and shells. I lay awake wondering where the next one would drop, and if the tanks had been observed. There is consolation in knowing that someone else is sharing the same discomfort as oneself. No sound came from the opposite shelf. In a low voice so as not disturb him if he were asleep, I said: "Are you awake, Gerry?" The reply came in no uncertain tones. "Am I awake? Humph! Who d'ye think could sleep through that?" Luckily there were no casualties from these nightly air-raids.

An observation balloon was moored near our field. One afternoon a squadron of enemy planes came unexpectedly into view out of a cloud. They attacked the balloon. The observer succeeded in escaping by means of his parachute. I watched his descent to safety as the balloon was riddled by machine-gun bullets.

In a far corner of our field there was a long-necked gun, familiarly known as "Pooping Peter." It was reputed to fire into Roulers, the headquarters of the opposing Army Commander. If the position of "Pooping Peter" was discovered, the Army Commander would see to it that our field became the target of the massed enemy guns. How we cursed it then each night, when it started firing! Not only did it keep us awake, but there was the danger that it would be located by the flash of each discharge.

From forward in the Salient on our way back to our dug-out each evening at dusk, we used to pass the men going up to the firing-line. They marched in single file along the side of the Menin road. Their sallow faces haunted me. For many it would be their last journey.

4

About October the 21st, after seventeen days in the Salient, we hoped to be sent to a rest camp at a small seaside town.

We were looking forward to the end of our fruitless labours, floundering in the mud round Ypres. Then there was a sudden reversal of plan.

Two tanks were to take part in an attack against Polderhoek Chateau, on the Passchendaele Ridge.

Gerrard had the unenviable honour of being chosen as the section commander to undertake the show, with Bown and Glanville in charge of the tanks. Two more capable tank commanders it would have been hard to find. Both had the highest ideals, and a strongly developed sense of duty. Bown was not yet twenty, a fresh-looking young fellow of hefty build. Glanville was about ten years older, neat and active. The tanks were to go along the Menin road. Almost at Gheluvelt, half-a-mile beyond the enemy line, they were to turn north across country. Polderhoek Chateau was situated on the high ground about half-a-mile away. It was in the neighbourhood of where Robertson had won his V.C., and the nature of both the operation and the ground was similar. It would be essential for Gerrard to lead his tanks on foot, to prevent their being ditched or losing direction once they were off the road.

There was a conference of officers, including some of the Staff, to discuss the plan of attack, Gerrard, of course, being present. The Colonel said he felt confident that any of his officers would be willing, like Captain Robertson, to make the supreme sacrifice, in order to secure the success of the attack.

When the conference ended the plan of attack had been arranged; but the date and hour had not yet been fixed. The Colonel shook hands with Gerrard as though in final good-bye, promising that his kit would be looked after.

With his two tank commanders Gerrard went

up to reconnoitre, and found that conditions were just about as bad as they could be. It was doubtful if the tanks could go into action even along the road, it was so badly broken by enormous holes. It was certain that as soon as the attack commenced the road would be shelled to blazes, and the odds were the tanks would be hit.

We appreciated the fire in our dug-out. It was the most cheerful thing in the Salient. In the evening after dinner we lay on our stretchers with the fire between us at our head. We reminisced, discussed and argued. Reputations were torn to shreds. Luckily, we found little fault with each other. If our opinions were too strongly divided, there was always the muddy ditch between us to restrain the ardour of our debate.

On the night of Tuesday, October the 23rd, we had turned in as usual, and the talk centred upon the proposed attack against Polderhoek Chateau— the matter uppermost in our mind. We were in entire agreement on this subject. It was damnable! Half-an-hour before midnight, a message came from the Company Commander that he wanted to see Gerrard at once. Gerrard hurriedly got ready and went off. I waited in suspense. About ten minutes later he returned with a set face. The attack on Polderhoek Chateau was fixed for daybreak twenty-four hours later. His orders were that this was an action where the section commander must lead his tanks from outside. I felt terribly sorry for Gerrard. There was no doubt in my mind that the attack meant certain death for him. We talked it over, and I was trying to be optimistic about his chances, when a second message came from the

Company Commander. This time for me! After putting on a few clothes, I went across the short distance to his quarters in an Armstrong hut in another part of the hedge, wondering what on earth I was going to be let in for. He gave me written orders. At six o'clock that morning I was to take two officers, and thirty men to repair about a mile of the Menin road, to enable Gerrard's tanks to get into action along it. The stretch of road mentioned in the orders was: "from HOOGE DUMP to crater beyond CLAPHAM JUNCTION." The equipment at my disposal was ten shovels, ten picks and two felling axes. The party was to carry haversack rations, and the job was to be finished that day. Pearson showed me on the map the task to be carried out, and told me to get detailed information from Gerrard regarding the particular places most in need of repair. This I knew already for Gerrard had described with a wealth of detail the condition of the road, and the swamp on each side of it, torn by shells and sodden with rain. When I got back to the dug-out and told Gerrard that I was for the "high-jump" too, he almost unconsciously cheered up. There is a Spanish proverb which says that: "The misfortune of others is the consolation of fools." Nevertheless, there *is* comfort in knowing that one is not marked out to be the sole victim. Though not as dangerous, we both knew that my job was as hopeless as his. The road was being shelled continually and its appearance changed, as fresh craters appeared in it from hour to hour.

When, following Pearson's instructions, I asked Gerrard to indicate the position of the worst parts of the road, he replied: "The whole bloody road is a succession of craters, and you'll have to repair it as best you can, if I am to get my tanks along it; but there are two big crumps you *can't* miss—one at HOOGE DUMP and the other just beyond CLAPHAM JUNCTION. Both stretch almost across the road. How you are going to fill them, I don't know." I knew that the job was impossible, and that it was useless to attempt it. But orders were orders, and I had to go forward as though believing it could be done.

I called at once for my section orderly, Bell, and told him to take the actual written orders I had received, to the two subalterns in question—"A" and "B"—at their dug-outs. Neither of them belonged to my section. I wanted them to know immediately of the job they were to do a few hours later.

Compared with what Gerrard and his two tank commanders had to do, our task was safe. The thought of possible danger did not trouble me; but what did worry me was how to tackle the job, and the fear that if I did not succeed the life of Gerrard and the others would be jeopardized. I had the faculty of being able to waken at any hour I wanted, and managed to get a couple of hours sleep.

At six o'clock the Sergeant-Major paraded twenty-six N.C.O.s and men, and my section orderly. The subalterns also reported to me. Spray was present to supervise the issue of the equipment. I warned officers and men with great emphasis that under no circumstances must they tell anyone of the reason for the work, nor mention a single word about an osprey operation which might take place. ("Osprey" was the code word for a tank.) I also told them how important it was that the work should be completed that day. There was to be no coming back until it was done. I impressed upon them the secrecy and urgency of the job. I indicated on the map to "A" and "B" the exact part of the road to be repaired, and mentioned it was about a mile in length. To avoid the risk of the whole party being blown up by a single shell, I decided to divide it into two at Birr X-Rd. I explained this to the two officers, and instructed "A" to commence work *at* Clapham Junction and work backwards. Clapham Junction was known as a tank cemetery because there were fully a dozen derelict tanks there. "B" was to start at Hooge Dump and work forward to meet "A". In that way the whole stretch of road would be covered. In case of shell-fire the parties might break off work and take cover. But in any case the work had to be finished that day.

We went to Birr X-Rd by lorry, arriving soon after 7 a.m. There was a considerable amount of movement on the road—lorries, limbers, pack-mules, and men. I divided the party in two. I thought it would be courting trouble to divide it equally, and give each officer thirteen men. So I gave fourteen to "A" and twelve to "B". My runner, Bell, remained with me. I explained to the officers that the stretch of road to be repaired lay farther along. I purposely sent "A's" party ahead as they had farthest to go, and said that as soon as I had got "B's" party started I would rejoin him, and we would investigate the crater on the spot. I gave

"B" his instructions, as, with his party we followed about 150 yards in the rear of "A's". In next to no time "A's" party became engulfed in the traffic and lost to view. I sent my runner to tell him to keep in touch with me. After a while Bell returned and said that he had not been able to find the party. In amazement I went forward at once, expecting every moment to overtake them. But I arrived at Clapham Junction without finding any trace of them. I went on eventually, getting into INVER-NESS COPSE. The road here was deserted. There was not a living soul to be seen. I suspected that our own front line was in this neighbourhood; but I could see no sign of it. The surface of the road was churned to mud. I passed a hand sticking up. Its owner had evidently been buried by a shell. I have since been told that this hand remained unburied because the troops going up into the line regarded it with superstitious reverence. They believed if they touched it, no harm would come to them. At the point I reached there was a water-filled crater stretching almost across the road. I presumed that this was the crump to which Gerrard had referred. Five or six tanks could have sunk in it easily. Floating on the surface of the water were several dead bodies. As I gazed forward across a black expanse of mud where no life was visible, the desolation of the scene reminded me of a cold grey sea and deserted shore.

I retraced my steps, searching both sides of the road, but without result. When I arrived back at Clapham Junction, I went some little way along the plank road to Polygone Wood, in case "A" had

F

followed it by mistake. Again I drew a blank. There were no men to be seen. There was an unnatural stillness all round. I went by the loop-way, south of Hooge, back to Birr X-Rd, wondering if "A", having lost touch with me, had returned that way. But again my luck was out. Once more I went back to Clapham Junction, but nowhere could I find the lost party. Of all the people I asked along the road none could give me any information. Hoping that "A" would find his way to Clapham Junction, I went back to help "B" and his squad. I had hardly rejoined them when, without the least warning, our guns commenced a terrific bombardment. The enemy soon retaliated, and we were caught in his barrage. The Menin road was going up in spouts of earth and smoke. If Gerrard's tanks were caught in a barrage like that they would be smashed to pieces. With one of the squad I was cut off from the remainder of the party. I waved and shouted to the men to take cover. The noise was ear-splitting. The shell-fire forced "B" and his men one way, and me and my companion another. We eventually took cover in a dug-out with some gunners. When gunners went to earth things were serious. From them I learnt it was a practice barrage our guns were putting over. With my inside knowledge, I realized it was a rehearsal for next morning's attack. The shelling was so intense that both my wrist watches stopped.

About a quarter-past-eleven the barrage had slightly abated, and I set out on a last search for "A" and his party, going along the Menin road right up to Inverness Copse again. Inquiries at dug-outs along the road elicited no information. "A" and his party seemed to have vanished off the face of the earth. I gave up my search in despair, and went to see how "B" was getting on. It only required a bombardment like the one we had just had to undo any work that had been done. Besides —the task was hopeless, for it would have required train loads of rubble to have made any appreciable difference to the surface of the road. Seeing that all had been done that could be done, I ordered everyone home. About one o'clock I reached camp myself and met Pearson outside his quarters. He looked very serious. I reported to him what had happened as far as I knew. Then he told me that "A" with all his men, except one, had been taken prisoner.

The party had missed its way and not seeing our front line, which had been withdrawn owing to the practice barrage, had walked on right into the enemy lines.

At first, the enemy was surprised, and thinking it was an attacking party had put up their hands. But when they saw that the "raiders" were armed only with shovels, picks and an axe, they had thrown hand grenades at them.

Although the written orders had been explicit regarding road-mending equipment and haversack rations, no mention had been made concerning the wearing of revolvers. Our men were, therefore, unarmed.

They had picked up the grenades before they exploded and had thrown them back. In the fight one man had been wounded, and had managed to escape by crawling away on his stomach, while

"A" and the other *thirteen* had been taken prisoners.

The enemy would now know from the badges of their prisoners that tanks were in the neighbourhood, and would expect a tank attack. There was, therefore, no hope of its success, and the plan was abandoned.

While we were on the Menin road, Gerrard's tanks had started to move up so that they should be well forward at night for the attack next morning. Many months later Glanville told me how when he was moving up with the tanks that morning, from Elton Point, the trees, the fields, the copses looked drab and miserable. But how when returning home from Valley Cottages, with the attack cancelled, and going through those same fields and copses and past the same trees, the whole world seemed bright and cheerful, and he saw things of beauty in nature which he had never noticed before.

By a strange coincidence, Polderhoek Chateau was captured in the first week of November without the aid of tanks, by a London battalion, in which Glanville's brother was the Stokes Gun Officer. In the attack he won the M.C. for the third time.

At four o'clock in the afternoon of the day of the road-repairing episode, I had to prepare a report. At five o'clock the following day I had to send in another report, and subsequently send in a statement for a Court of Inquiry to be held on the instructions of the Army Commander. The Court of Inquiry sat on the 31st of October. "B" corroborated the orders I had given "A". His evidence, together with the statement of the man who had escaped, resulted in the court completely exonerating me from any blame. On the contrary, the precautions I had taken against shell-fire in dividing up the party, were commended, and I was congratulated both by the Colonel and General Courage on the way I had handled the affair. Some stinging comments were made on the fact that the men had not been issued with revolvers and ammunition, and that tank men had been sent up to do the job of a labour gang.

General Courage was my General during the whole of my service with the tanks in Flanders and France. I valued the appreciation he accorded me on this occasion. It was in keeping with his character. He never grudged encouragement. He was fair in his judgments, and gave a pat on the back when he thought a thing well done. He demanded good work from his officers, and saw that he got it. His shattered lower jaw bore witness to his distinguished war record.

A day or two before the Court of Inquiry, I brought "Huguenot" and "Hermosa" back to Elton Point. As "Hermosa" was going through Ypres, an official photographer took a photo of her. I believe I came into the picture. But it was taken without my knowing. I was in full active service kit, complete with tin hat, gas appliances, trench coat, and heavy field boots, all well caked with mud, quite in keeping with the conditions round about Ypres.

At the end of October, the tanks started to leave the Salient. Even on the return trip from Voormezeele to Ouderdoom, one tank of the battalion was badly ditched in a swamp. It defied all efforts to get it out, and sank until it was half-filled with water. After two days it was hauled out by another tank.

We entrained at Ouderdoom on Thursday, November the 1st, exactly four weeks to the day after our arrival. Our destination was Montenescourt, five miles west of Arras, so we were looking forward to having a "cushy" time.

It was without regret that we left the Salient.

The historian, Captain B. H. Liddell Hart, in his book *THE REAL WAR, 1914-1918*, says: "Thus, when on 4th November, a sudden advance by the 1st Division and 2nd Canadian Division gained the empty satisfaction of occupying the site of Passchendaele village, the official curtain was at last rung down on the pitiful tragedy of 'Third Ypres.' It was the long overdue close of a campaign which had brought the British Armies to the verge of exhaustion, one in which had been enacted the most dolorous scenes in British military history, and for which the only justification evolved the reply that, in order to absorb the enemy's attention and forces, Haig chose the spot most difficult for himself and least vital to his enemy. Intending to absorb the enemy's reserves, his own were absorbed. . . .

"The only relief to this sombre review is that a bare fortnight later was enacted, on a different stage, with a technique suggested in early August, a 'curtain-raiser' which was to be developed into the glorious drama of autumn, 1918."

# CHAPTER IV

## CAMBRAI. THE SECTION CAPTURES FONTAINE-NOTRE-DAME, THE APEX OF THE THRUST

### I

THE rest we had been expecting about October the 21st, was now materialising, only better than we had hoped for. We were heading towards our Winter Quarters. The tanks trekked from Montenescourt, across fields of peaceful country, keeping parallel to the road. We stopped the night at the little village of Avesnes-le-Comte, where I was billeted at a mediæval inn. We messed at a private house in the village, where Madame and her daughter provided us with a substantial meal, typical *cuisine française*. Twenty to thirty of us squeezed round a large table, with Pearson at the head. The room was full of hungry officers. Madame waited at table, keeping up an animated running commentary. She said that she was "Maman" of this big family of *garçons bien élevés*. Then turning to Pearson, who had been giving some instructions, she remarked that he was "Papa." He was young, and had been busy to have such a large family. Pearson, who was not yet thirty and had been recently married, seemed to find it difficult to appreciate her humour. It was obvious that he was rather annoyed at the amusement it caused. This kind of thing was bad for discipline. She hastened to soothe his offended dignity by saying it was only her "badinage." After all one must smile—*la guerre c'est terrible!*

After dinner I returned to my ancient hostelry, where I had been given a room with an enormous four-poster bed. Compared with the hardships of the Salient, it seemed the acme of comfort, with its spotless sheets of cambric linen. I sank luxuriously into the soft feather-bed, amused at the novelty of having a second feather-bed on top of me. An atmosphere of peace and solitude pervaded the old bedchamber with its antique furniture. I wondered as I lay there whether centuries ago this room had sheltered a knight, who had, perhaps, given his name to the village.

The tanks resumed their trek next morning, and reached Bois de Faye, near Bavincourt, some eight miles west of Montenescourt. This was a rather longer trek than usual for tanks, and we wondered how the sprockets and rollers would stand the wear and tear of the journey. My tanks were parked in a small clearing in the wood, and we camped in tents and bivouacs in the lee of the tanks. The weather was wet and clammy; but by this time we had learnt to make ourselves comfortable in a Robinson Crusoe way.

For the next five days we did not bother about the future. We did not know where we were going; but all that mattered was that we were away from the bombs and the shells. We believed that this was a step towards our Winter Quarters, and, in the meantime, we enjoyed the rustic peace of the undisturbed countryside. It was not only a blessed relief to be enveloped in a silence which could almost be heard, but to be able to feast one's eyes upon the auburn tints of the autumn foliage. In the Argentine the landscape is featureless—flat prairie (the "pampas") stretching to the horizon on all sides. Because of this, I suppose, I had never taken to camp life. Now, after the desolation of the Salient, I felt to my surprise, an understanding of the beauty of nature stealing over me. I began to realize how lucky and happy we all really were before the interminable War started.

Just before this, I had lost my senior tank commander, the Honourable Cecil Edwardes, who had been promoted and put in command of a section in another company. "Hermosa" was now taken over by Keay, a full lieutenant, and the crew remained the same.

At Bois de Faye the sections worked and messed separately, so that I no longer saw so much of Gerrard.

It was not until a week after leaving the Salient that we were disillusioned, and learned that our "cushy" time was at an end. The whole of the Tank Corps was to go into action. The place itself was not stated; but we knew that the tanks were to be given an opportunity to prove their worth on firm, suitable ground. If they failed this time they were done for. The whole plan had been prepared with the greatest secrecy, and special tactics for the tanks co-operating with the infantry had been evolved. We were to rehearse with the infantry over a model battle-field which had been prepared. A feature of the attack was the use of a new device called a "fascine." This consisted of an enormous bundle of brushwood bound by strong chains. It was as wide as the tank, about four feet in diameter, and about one and a half tons in weight. Each tank was to carry one of these on its cabin. The fascine was released from inside the tank and dropped forward into a trench which was too wide and deep for the tank to cross in the ordinary way. By crossing over on the fascine, the tank now could negotiate the trench successfully.

The model battle-field had three rows of trenches to be crossed, the first preceded by an area of dense barbed wire. The tanks were to advance by sections in spear-head formation. The one at the point of the spear-head was called the "advance guard tank," and the other two were known as "main body tanks."

In previous battles there had always been a preliminary bombardment to cut away the wire. The grave disadvantage of this method was that it gave the enemy warning of an attack, and he was consequently prepared. The essence of this particular action was to be surprise. There would be no preliminary bombardment, and the tanks were to replace the artillery in cutting down the wire.

The advance guard tank went forward crushing a path in the wire until it reached the first trench, when it turned left and fired into the trench to keep down the heads of the enemy. In the meantime, the two main body tanks made for a point in the first trench. The left one of these tanks dropped its fascine into the trench, crossed over it, and turned left along the trench. The right one also crossed on the same fascine, and made for a point in the second trench. There it dropped its own fascine, and crossed over on it, then turning left. Meanwhile, the advance guard tank crossed over the first trench on the fascine used by the two main body tanks, went over the fascine dropped in the second trench, and on to the third trench, where it dropped its own fascine and crossed over. The two main body tanks followed the advance guard tank on the fascines already laid. This ingenious method was the most economical way of using the fascines, for each section of three tanks crossed three trenches on three fascines. The infantry followed through the paths cut in the wire by the tanks.

Even all these preparations left us in the dark as to where the battle was to take place.

At one of the rehearsals I met, by chance, Rowbotham, Junior, a subaltern. He had been at school with me in the Argentine, and we had not seen each other since then. He told me that his elder brother, who had also been a school-fellow of mine there, was a Lieutenant-Colonel, with the D.S.O. and M.C., in command of a Scottish infantry battalion.

To conform with the plan of spear-head formation, sections were now to consist of only three tanks, instead of four. In our Company each of the three fighting sections gave up its fourth tank, which was handed over to the supply section under Edwards (the "Dishonourable"). The decision as to which tank with its officer and crew, was to be handed over was a delicate matter. One could not help having preferences, and the natural tendency was to keep one's strongest tanks oneself. After consideration I decided to part with "Huguenot." "Hadrian" and "Havoc" were male tanks; "Hermosa" and "Huguenot," females. My preference was for keeping the male tanks with the 6-pounders. Therefore, it was a question of discarding one of the female tanks. "Hermosa" was under the command of Keay, a full lieutenant, while McAllister, a second lieutenant, was in charge of "Huguenot." I naturally chose to keep the senior lieutenant. Though, I must confess, in addition, I could not drag myself to part with "Hermosa," for I, like the Honourable Cecil Edwardes, had a love for this name on account of my association with Latin-America. I had been studying for an honours degree in Spanish when I received my commission, and this Spanish word was for me a connecting link between my former and my present life. McAllister was very sick at being pushed out of the section, and I was sorry to lose him and a fine crew.

After three or four days of rehearsals, we returned to Montenescourt, where the tanks were overhauled. The only repair needed was the shortening of the tracks by taking out a plate. The tracks had stretched with use. This stretching was a normal occurrence, and allowance up to a limit could be made for it by adjustment. When the limit was reached, the track was shortened by the removal of a plate. It was only now that each of our tanks received its own fascine.

Round about the 14th of November we left Montenescourt. By night the tanks crawled on to

a train there, each tank bearing its grotesque bundle
on its head; but once on its own truck the tank had
to deposit the fascine on the floor of the truck, for
otherwise it would have fouled bridges over the
railway line. This increased enormously the
difficulties of entrainment.

We were off for an unknown destination.

2

Throughout that night and all next day we were
in the train. We had no means of judging how
much farther we had to go. There were long halts;
but as we were obviously in rear areas and making
a detour, the slow railway journey was treated as
a sight-seeing excursion. After an extra long halt
at a railway-junction, we were told that rail-head
was at Ytres. We arrived there in the dead of
night. The distance between Montenescourt and
Ytres was only twenty-three miles as the crow flies,
yet we had taken about twenty-four hours to make
the journey.

The tanks were detrained without eventuality,
each with its fascine. In the darkness they moved
up the three-and-a-half miles from rail-head to
Dessart Wood, which lay about four miles behind
the front line. From its appearance it might have
been out of the War zone, for it still really was a
wood. There was thick undergrowth which made
going on foot difficult. In the pitch darkness, it
was no easy matter to get the tanks into the interior
without their blazing a trail which in daylight might
betray their presence. As far as possible all traces

of the marks of the tracks entering the wood were obliterated, and the machines themselves were camouflaged among the trees, which afforded splendid cover from aerial observation. We made our quarters in bivouacs and inside the tanks. A very comfortable shelter could be contrived under the nose of a tank, or with a ground-sheet stretched like an awning from the side of the tank. As at Bois de Faye, the Company was decentralized, and the sections worked and messed independently. The cooks had to exercise their ingenuity to make fires without smoke. An amazing feature of the wood was that it was literally strewn with hundreds of horseshoes. For this obvious reason we rechristened it "Horseshoe Wood."

The plan for the battle was now explained to us.

It was well considered, having been sanctioned by G.H.Q. as far back as the 20th October, when "Z" day had been fixed for a month ahead— the 20th of November. I now realized that when the rumour was spread that we were leaving the Salient for a rest camp near the seaside, it was all part of the scheme for secrecy.

In point of fact, on the 5th August a plan for a raid by tanks had been placed before General Byng by a tank officer. "Byng was receptive to the idea," to use the words of Captain Liddell Hart in *The Real War, 1914-1918*, "although inclined to expand it from a raid into a break-through attack to gain Cambrai. Next day he went to General Headquarters, saw Haig, and suggested a surprise attack with tanks at Cambrai in September. The Commander-in-Chief was favourable, but his Chief

of Staff, General Kiggell, offered strong objections
on the ground that the Army could not win a
decisive battle in two places at once, and should
rather concentrate every possible man in the Ypres
Sector . . . Thus the enlarged idea helped to post-
pone the raid, as the refusal to recognize reality at
Ypres postponed the attack at Cambrai until too
late for decisive results to be possible.

"The historian, while respecting Kiggell's
emphasis on the principle of concentration, may
doubt whether Ypres was a suitable site for the
fulfilment of this principle, and may also hold that
distraction of the enemy's force has been an
essential complement to concentration—of one's
own effort.

"Kiggell's objections sufficed to dissuade Haig,
who still valued the tank as only 'a minor factor.'
Thus the Cambrai project was postponed inde-
finitely while the High Command persevered with
their hopeless efforts in the Passchendaele swamps."

The object of the attack was the smashing of
the "Hindenburg Line," which the enemy was
reputed to hold lightly, believing it to be impreg-
nable without weeks of preliminary bombardment
to cut away the huge belts of wire in front, during
which time he would bring up troops to withstand
the attack. The possibility of a sudden tank attack
was ruled out. The Hindenburg trenches were so
deep and wide that no existing tank could cross
them without becoming ditched in the attempt.
Our model battle-field at Bavincourt had been a
replica of a section of the Hindenburg defences.
The ground we were to traverse was chalky downs
of firm undulating grassland and ideal going for

tanks. The prestige and very existence of the Tank Corps was at stake.

My own personal feeling was that I wanted to go into action inside a tank; but I did want it to be under conditions which would give the tank a fair chance. The preparations had been perfectly thought out, and it seemed to me that as long as the enemy had not got wind of the project, the attack would be a walk-over. If he had, however, he would be prepared with light guns in forward areas, machine-guns with armour-piercing bullets, tank traps, and extra troops, so that the operation might end in disaster, and put "paid" to the Tank Corps. The whole Corps was being risked in this one hazardous operation to prove the worth of the tank. The fascine itself had never been tested in battle. Without it the whole project was impossible.

Grounds, who was well up in the geography of the British front, remarked that if the Hindenburg defences were smashed, the cavalry would probably sweep through to Cambrai—a vital railway junction. If the Germans lost Cambrai, they would have to withdraw over a wide area, for their existing front line could not be maintained without it. Should that happen, it might mean the *guerre finie!*

We were all keyed up and anxious that the action should be an unqualified success. We liked to think that the horseshoes abounding in the wood were good omens.

For the next four days the wood was a hive of subdued industry. The crews were busy getting the tanks into perfect trim—oiling, greasing and making any necessary adjustment. The tracks were fitted with "spuds," to enable them to get a grip on the ground. These were much on the same principle as studs and ribs on football boots, and were clipped on at regular intervals. The crews, also, had to get the tanks completely loaded. A "tank-fill" consisted of 60 gallons of petrol, 10 gallons of oil, 20 gallons of water, 10 lbs. of grease, 10,000 rounds of S.A. ammunition for a female tank, or 200 rounds of 6-pounder ammunition and 6,000 rounds of S.A. ammunition for a male, in addition to food supplies and fresh water. The officer held in reserve privately a bottle of whisky in his locker; also a bottle of rum, saved up from the unused rations of men who would not touch it.

Our "point of assembly" for the attack was to be just south of the village of Beaucamp, four miles distant. The Company Reconnaissance Officer prepared a route up to it for our tanks. The route lay across undulating green fields, between Havrincourt Wood and Gouzeaucourt Wood. I went over it several times to get the lie of the land photographed on my brain. We were to go up at night, and it was my responsibility to get my three tanks to the point of assembly at the correct time. My father was a stickler for thoroughness. He had always demanded it of me, so that it was now second nature to me.

About five o'clock, after darkness had fallen, on Monday, the 19th of November, we left Dessart Wood on our "approach march" to Beaucamp. A white tape, about two inches wide with a black line along the centre, had been laid over the whole

G

distance. The officer walked in front of his tank to be able to see the tape and direct the driver, guiding him by the glow of a cigarette. A tank was not allowed to go astride the tape for fear of ripping it up. For some considerable distance the tape remained intact, and was of great assistance. Then it ended abruptly. It was quite impossible to direct the tanks by the lie of the country, for the night was pitch black and no landmarks were visible. There were several breaks like this where the tape had been ripped up. On these occasions I walked ahead trying to pick out the track marks of a preceding tank. At times it was difficult to pick even these out by the light of a cigarette and I had to use my electric torch. During the approach march the front in our sector was ominously quiet. The previous night the enemy had raided our line and captured prisoners. Did the silence mean that the secret was out? I was so busy getting my tanks up that I had no time to worry about that. About midnight we reached our jumping-off place, taking up a position behind a hedge. The four miles of approach march had taken in the darkness seven hours—an average speed of little more than half-a-mile an hour! The rollers of the tanks were greased up, and the tanks were left ready for action, when the men turned in to snatch a few hours' sleep inside the tanks.

We were on the eve of the first great tank battle, the battle of Cambrai. My three officers, Second-Lieutenant G. D. Hardy ("Hadrian"), Second-Lieutenant K. E. Hughes ("Havoc"), and Lieutenant S. G. Keay ("Hermosa"), were all younger than I, and I was twenty-two years old.

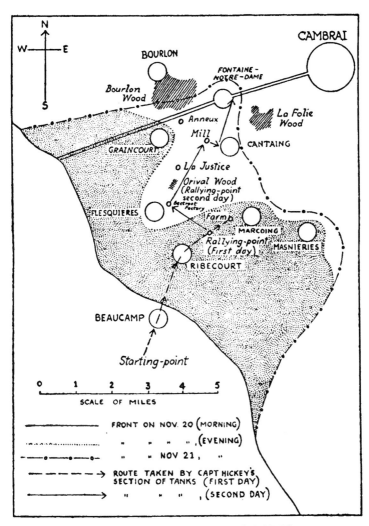

THE THRUST TOWARDS CAMBRAI

## 3

A section commander's job was to be where he could be of most use to the infantry while still keeping control of his tanks. I attached myself to "Hadrian," as that was the advance guard tank of my section. It was to be followed by "Hermosa," as No. 1 main-body, and "Havoc," as No. 2. My idea was that the female tank should be between the males to get the protection of their 6-pounders.

In "Hadrian" at an early hour, sausages were sizzling on a Primus stove, on the platform behind the engine, and mugs of hot tea were handed round. At ten minutes past six, the tanks with their engines running as silently as possible, started to move forward very slowly and with the minimum of noise. Ten minutes later (6.20 a.m.) was "Zero hour," when the barrage commenced. The guns reverberated like incessant thunderclaps. Our first bump came fairly soon. We climbed a bank, crashed through the hedge on top, and came down heavily on the other side. The perfect tank driver would balance his tank on the top of an ascent, and let it down gently at just the right moment. But even perfect tank drivers got excited, and it was a good thing—since a tank had no springs—that its maximum speed was only three miles an hour. When it lurched it threw its crew about like so many pea-nuts, and they had to clutch on to whatever they could when we were going over uneven ground. Any bit of equipment not in its place, clattered about, making a noise like a can on a dog's tail.

Our "starting line" was the British support trench in front of Beaucamp, and we were to be there half-an-hour after zero. On our way down the slope, in the dull, grey light, we had a thrilling and extensive view of the battle. The enemy had been taken completely by surprise and the sky in front was lit by his coloured S.O.S. lights. It was a weird but impressive sight! The whole corps of 350 tanks was taking part. We were in the third wave and right in the centre of the battle-line. As far as the eye could see, monstrous tanks, like pre-historic animals, each carrying an enormous bundle of brushwood on its head, were advancing relent-lessly. The first two waves of tanks, with their infantry following, were well forward. Ahead of us, the General himself (General Elles, commanding the Tank Corps) with head and shoulders sticking out of the top manhole of his flag-tank, "Hilda," led the attack.

My Section crossed the front line at a quarter-past seven, and the infantry, with whom we were to co-operate, followed the two main-body tanks from there, at a distance of about seventy yards. Utterly bewildered, the enemy was surrendering in panic in all directions. The noise inside "Hadrian" was deafening; it almost drowned the noise of the barrage, and speech was practically impossible. I was in the left gangway to keep in touch with Hardy, the tank commander. The rattle of the tracks and machinery produced the illusion of tremendous speed; but we were not moving faster than a mile an hour. As we clattered across "No Man's Land," following a course parallel to the road from Beaucamp to Ribécourt, shells from a single enemy gun were whizzing past us and falling among the infantry, who suffered several casualties. Their company commander was killed outright by one of these shells. It was peculiar to see spouts of earth rising from the ground and not hear the shells bursting about 150 yards away. The noise surrounding one inside the tank completely drowned the sound of the explosions at that distance. Then a machine-gun started; the rain of bullets on the right side of the tank was like the tapping of innumerable small hammers. I had left the sponson door on my side open, so that I could see how the infantry were following my two main-body tanks. A side glance through the doorway gave me a sudden shock. There was a British soldier lying face downward, dead, his inert body twisted. It seemed already slightly swollen. Any minute one of us might come to a similar glorious, but not particularly desirable, end. Now—ten minutes after we had crossed our front line—frantic signs from the infantry behind warned us that there was something wrong on top of the tank. We had reached the barbed-wire before the German advance trench, and bits of it were pulled up by the tracks. They had caught in the camouflage net, and were dragging it off. We managed to get the net freed without casualties, during a brief interval when the firing ceased. At the same time, I discovered that the sponson door was being jammed by the wire. After that I took care to keep it closed.

When we reached the Hindenburg main trench some ten minutes later, the tank was surrounded by groups of the enemy eager to surrender themselves and their arms. There flashed across my mind the scene at Las Palmas, when the local vendors in small open boats surged round the liner, endeavouring to sell their wares. One Jerry tried to hand his rifle through the front port-hole; but we were not collecting souvenirs, and directed him and his companions to go further on to the infantry. We crossed the Hindenburg main and reserve trenches according to plan. The fascines were a great success; and the infantry were able to advance through the gaps which the tanks had made in crushing their way over the fifty yards of dense, barbed-wire.

We had pushed through the first two waves. They were consolidating the positions they had captured. Now when we started to go over as yet untraversed ground, our job really began. There was a congestion of traffic on the road outside Ribécourt, and we had to take our turn in the queue of tanks of the third wave, waiting to enter the village. We were on the lookout for snipers in windows and doorways, and as a minatory gesture fired several shots into the houses. But the place was apparently deserted. The enemy had evidently beaten a hasty retreat. Our objective was a section of the Hindenburg Support System, lying beyond this village. After passing through its south-east corner, we found that we could not make direct for our objective. We were separated from it by the embankment of the railway running from Ribécourt to Marcoing. In descending a steep slope on to a light railway on the near side of the main line, our tank bumped heavily, and its fascine broke loose at the back and fell off. We crossed

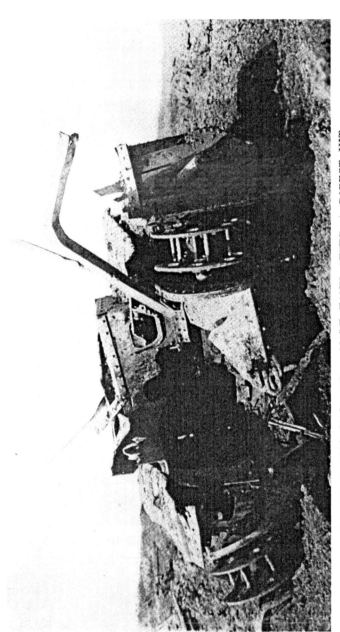

ALL THAT WAS LEFT OF A MALE TANK AFTER A DIRECT HIT

the Hindenburg Support System on the near side of the railway, keeping on the road across which the trenches had not been dug, so we did not need the fascines. The railway embankment was here comparatively low, and we decided to go over it. The lines might break or crack a plate or two of the tracks, but we would risk that. Carefully and slowly the tank was driven over each rail, without mishap. On the far side a white deal table freshly scrubbed had been left out to dry, and a bicycle was resting against it. This was indeed evidence of the enemy's hasty evacuation. Because of our detour we arrived at the far side of the particular trench sector that we were to attack. However, that did not matter, because we found it deserted. We sent off a carrier pigeon with news that we had gained our objective.

Encouraged by our success, we clattered across the fields in the direction of Marcoing. Just over half-way there we came across a farm-house. It was a target not to be missed. The three tanks opened fire on it, and disturbed a nest of machine-guns. After a short bombardment, one German officer and about twenty other ranks ran out, scattering in all directions. A number were successfully dealt with by our machine-guns; but one, lying flat on the ground, appeared to be feigning dead. The tank driver—Corporal Dunn—thought he saw the fellow move. It looked suspicious. A hand-grenade thrown against a track of the tank, would probably damage a plate and, if it broke it, put the tank out of action. The front machine-gun had got a stoppage, and would not work. Hardy pulled out his revolver, and the tank was driven

towards the miserable victim. He lay so still that
Hardy thought he really was dead. Dunn, however, looking through the port-hole in front of him,
exclaimed: "No, sir, he's not; I saw him blink. I'm
sure he's got a bomb in his hand." I took a look
through the front revolver loop-hole in the left
sponson. The man was elderly, short and thickly
set. He was lying right in front of the tank, and
almost on his face. His short, thick neck was
wrinkled and weather-beaten. I closed the flap,
and the report of Hardy's revolver ended the
incident.

The three tanks now separated to clear the
neighbourhood. "Hadrian" reached the outskirts
of Marcoing; but as we met with no resistance, at
about eleven o'clock I gave the return signal.

I walked outside "Hadrian," and was surprised
to see Hughes escorting a bunch of prisoners at the
point of his revolver. Single bullets swished past
me, and I noticed that each time Hughes and his
prize made a simultaneous genuflexion. The farm
evidently still contained a sniper; he was eventually
disposed of.

Later I heard what had happened. Hughes,
on the way back from Marcoing had, with his
corporal, entered a German dug-out, and captured
five prisoners, some arms and ammunition. Fifteen
minutes later, he had bagged four more prisoners
who were attempting to escape in the direction of
Marcoing, and shortly after that had captured a
German officer. The whole lot he had handed over
to our infantry. It was while he was marching
them back that I had seen him.

On our return journey we had the unpleasant

experience of being shelled by a field-gun. Fortunately the shells went high, and we escaped a direct hit by taking cover in a fold in the ground. A low-flying aeroplane was evidently hit by accident and fell in flames some little distance away. For the Battle of Cambrai the Royal Flying Corps had adopted new tactics. They were deliberately flying low to co-operate with the advancing tanks and infantry.

By one o'clock my Section was back at the Company rallying-point, near Ribécourt.

Of Gerrard's three tanks, two had been disabled and the third, Glanville's, had been hit by an enemy light gun, which had also knocked out other tanks on the Flesquières ridge. It was probably the same gun, or a gun of the same battery, that had fired at my tanks on their return from Marcoing.

Using the long grass for cover, Glanville had crept towards a gun east of the village of Flesquières in action against the tanks topping the ridge, and with a Lewis gun taken from his tank had scattered the crew. This may have been the field gun which was reputed to have been served single-handed by the legendary German artillery officer, whose great bravery was mentioned by Sir Douglas Haig in his Cambrai Dispatch, but about whom the Germans make no claim. There were anything up to ten men serving the gun that Glanville put out of action. The German artillery officer *mentioned* by Sir Douglas Haig would certainly appear to belong to fiction, for the Germans themselves say*: "The fame of the unknown

---

*Royal Tank Corps Journal*, March, 1933, "A Cambrai Myth?" by Lieutenant-Colonel F. E. Hotblack.

artillery officer will not be lessened if one allots the praise, which the enemy's commander bestowed upon one individual, to all the German batteries at Flesquières. Officers, N.C.O.s and gunners all contributed to an outstanding achievement."

It is evident that there were many enemy guns in action in the Flesquières ridge area. A German History gives the reason for the great artillery strength there: prisoners (a sergeant and several privates of an Irish regiment) had been captured just before the 20th November on this front, and they had been unanimous in their statements that tanks had come into the area, and that on the 20th there was to be an English attack in the Havrincourt salient. The German Higher Command could not believe, however, that we could attack without a long preliminary bombardment.

The Honourable Cecil Edwardes had reached his objective in his tank. Gerrard had gone up and spoken to him as he sat in his seat. Edwardes said he was thirsty and would like a drink of water. While Gerrard was away getting it a shell penetrated the tank from the front. It did not explode, but, passing between Edwardes and the tank driver without touching either of them, pushed back the engine of the tank. Edwardes died instantaneously of shock through heart-failure. Gerrard, on his return with the water, found him dead, sitting upright in the officer's seat with his pockets already rifled.

From all accounts, the battle had been the vindication of the Tank Corps. The tanks had proved their real worth, and succeeded beyond the most sanguine expectations. The enemy was on the run for the first time in the history of the War.

## 4

During the afternoon, I saw my tanks were greased and filled up from the supplies which Edwards' (the "Dishonourable") Section had brought up on sledges drawn behind the tanks. They had come up in the rear of the third wave. Before nightfall my Section was ready for any further move.

Next morning at half-past ten, the Company was told to move up to the Beetroot Factory at Flesquières, to get further orders. An hour later we started. Of the Company's twelve tanks, Gerrard's Section had been disabled or knocked out; of Edwards' Supply Section, only one tank was ready, as they had not anticipated having to go into action. My Section started off in the rear of Grounds's. Unfortunately, we went slightly off our course, which delayed our arrival at the rendezvous. On our way, we saw the tanks which had been knocked out the day before, as they topped the Flesquières ridge. They lay there in the form of a crescent—I did not count them; but I believe there were anything up to eighteen of them—some with enormous holes blown in their sides and fronts. One or two were a shapeless mass of metal. There is no doubt that there were at least three, and probably four, batteries of German artillery, which between them did this damage; one at the east of Flesquières would be the one which had knocked out the tanks which we now saw nearest to us on the ridge. As I walked beside the tanks, I wondered if our amazing good luck of the previous day would still hold. Then I caught sight of a grey object slightly ahead. It was the body of a German who had been terribly wounded in the abdomen. His hands were clasped in an agonized attempt to hold the rent together. I quickly averted my eyes, and thought: "There but for the grace of God lies Dan Hickey." As we trekked along we saw on our right, tanks in action against the village of Cantaing.

At the Beetroot Factory we got orders from Pearson to attack the village of Fontaine-Notre-Dame, just this side of Cambrai, and hold it until the infantry took over. I asked Pearson in whose tank he was going, so that I should know where to find him, and he replied he would follow up outside. The only other section commander taking part in the attack was Grounds, who was going inside "Harlequin." There was a ridge to be crossed before we reached Fontaine, and since we had already seen the mess that the enemy had made of tanks as they topped a ridge, we didn't feel too comfortable about it—especially as we now knew he was prepared for tanks. At half-past one seven tanks were drawn up in a line, at about 200 yards' interval, as though for a race. It was a clear, cold winter afternoon when we went into action for the second time in forty-eight hours. The first half-hour was uneventful and we rolled on comfortably over firm, smooth ground. After passing a farm-house at La Justice, on our left, Hardy, peering through his front port-hole, shouted: "See them running like rabbits!" The enemy had seen the tanks approaching and were beating a strategic retreat. Then we came to a sunken road which was so deep that Hardy was doubtful if he could negotiate it.  I got out of "Hadrian" and walked along the road to find a shallow place to cross. Having found a suitable spot, I got into "Hadrian" again, and we crossed without difficulty.  On the other side we were told by some Highlanders, of the 51st Division, that they were being held up by intense machine-gun fire from Cantaing Mill, and the trench system on either side of it.  This Division had been* "given the most important task of pushing right through to Cantaing and Fontaine-Notre-Dame, to open a way for the cavalry, who were to exploit the break-through. . . .  A Squadron of the Queen's Bays had come up and were awaiting developments, but the advance had come to a standstill.  Enemy aeroplanes flew low over the ranks lying extended in the open and poured machine-gun fire on them.

"This part of the chalk region of Artois, which resembles the down country in the south of England, had gone out of cultivation.  The ground rises slightly for about 200 yards in front of La Justice, and then a long spur runs in the direction of Fontaine, which itself lies on slightly rising ground beyond a shallow valley.  The valley marks the line of the main Bapaume-Cambrai road, which at this point crossed the front diagonally.  On the left towers Bourlon Wood; on the right, beyond Cantaing, and facing Bourlon Wood, lies La Folie Wood, also in German occupation. The distance to Fontaine-Notre-Dame is 4,000 yards over ground exposed to fire from the front and from both flanks. . . .

*A History of the Fourth Battalion the Seaforth Highlanders, by Lieutenant-Colonel M. M. Haldane.  Also, extracts which follow are from same source.

"At about noon tanks appeared, advancing on the right, and, under orders from Corps Headquarters, the Officers Commanding the 4th Seaforths and 7th Argyll and Sutherland, who had established joint headquarters in La Justice Farm, sent up orders for the advance to be resumed, but whether or not they reached the front line before the tanks is doubtful."

After a short bombardment by the tanks, the Highlanders were able to advance. They reported that the village contained machine-guns and snipers, so we went towards it, and worked round its southern edge. We helped them to retake it, and kept up machine-gun fire on the retreating enemy.

Now we turned towards the ridge which lay between us and Fontaine. The deviation to Cantaing had delayed us half-an-hour. We saw a tank of another battalion which had been knocked out earlier, and was still blazing furiously. Evidently there was artillery on the other side of the ridge. When we reached the top of it we found ourselves in the thick of a bombardment. Two enemy batteries of field-guns were blazing at the advancing tanks, one from the S.E. edge of Bourlon Wood and the other from near Fontaine church, and "the village was covered by a line of machine-guns, posted along its outer edge." "Hermosa" had taken a more direct route to Fontaine and was out of sight. One of the crew at the rear reported that "Havoc" was following, but that "Hydra" and "Harlequin" were knocked out. They had been "put out of action by direct hits when crossing the sunken road running from La

Justice to Cantaing" by two field-guns in Cantaing Mill, which were captured as the advance swept on. All I could see through a revolver loop-hole was Viveash's tank "Hong Kong" slightly ahead and about 200 yards to our left. She was coming in for the concentrated fury of the guns. Breathless, we watched her zig-zag as the shells dropped nearer and nearer. Clouds of earth flew up like water-spouts, some so close that a dozen times we thought she'd been hit. For the moment we were safe, but we realized that whether she got through or not, in a minute or so we should be going through the same hell. Hardy gave orders to keep on changing direction. Miraculously, "Hong Kong" escaped and charged down the slope into the valley. It was our turn now! Shells were bursting all round us, and fragments of them were striking the sides of the tank. While the four gunners blazed away, the rest of the perspiring crew kept the tank zig-zagging, to upset the enemy's aim. (It was a hard job to turn one of these early tanks. It needed four of the crew to work the levers, and they took their orders by signals. First of all, the tank had to stop. A knock on the right side would attract the attention of the right gearsman. The driver would hold out a clenched fist, which was the signal to put the track into *neutral*. The gearsman would repeat the signal to show it was done. The officer, who controlled two brake levers, would pull on the right one, which held the right track. The driver would accelerate, and the tank would slew round slowly on the stationary right track while the left track went into motion. As soon as the tank had turned sufficiently the procedure was

H

reversed. Zig-zagging was, therefore, a slow and complicated business.) In between pulls on his brakes, Hardy fired the front machine-gun. Our only hope of salvation was to keep going and to follow as erratic a course as possible. Just at this critical moment the "auto-vac," supplying petrol to the engine, failed. The engine spluttered and stopped. We were now a stationary target, incapable of moving one way or another. In the sudden silence we could hear the thud, thud of falling shells, and metal and earth striking the sides of the tank. Any moment it would be kingdom come! Automatically, I tightened my tin-hat, and adjusted my metal mask, with the feeling of: "Those about to die, salute thee, O Cæsar!" The atmosphere in the tank was foul. To the heat and smell of the engine were added cordite fumes, and the fact that nine men had been confined in this small space for close on three hours. It was a trying moment! With tense faces the crew watched the imperturbable second-driver as he coolly and methodically put the "auto-vac" right, ignoring all the proffered advice to give it a good hard knock. To the adjurations to hurry up or the tank would be blown to blazes, he replied with his habitual stutter: "Why d-don't you m-mind your own b-bloody b-business?"

Across the valley, set serenely on a slight rise, was Fontaine-Notre-Dame with its peaceful roofs and spire silhouetted against the evening sky. It must have been only a matter of minutes before we got started again, but it seemed a life-time! How we weren't hit during that brief period Providence alone knows! Then, down the slope we charged in "top" speed, with guns blazing, and the enemy batteries ceased firing. "The tanks advanced straight for the village and then wheeled along it, firing into it and silencing the machine-guns. But an advance of 4,000 yards under concentrated rifle fire from all sides had sadly depleted" the advancing infantry. "Captain 'Ray' Macdonald (Seaforths) himself fell, mortally wounded, forty yards ahead of his Company, whilst still three or four hundred yards from the village; but, fired by his splendid example, the gallant remnant pressed on until the village was reached."

The gunloader to Sergeant Mitchell was terribly keen to have a share in the firing. He begged Mitchell to let him have a "go". Permission being given, he asked Hardy if he could have a shot at the spire of Fontaine church, suggesting that there might be an observer there. Hardy, disliking the idea of the wanton destruction of a church, said: "No!" Once at the gun, the enthusiast started firing at such a pace that after a short while he collapsed in a state of utter exhaustion.

Twilight was falling and there was a mist rising from the ground as we reached the outskirts of the village, which we scoured for half-an-hour without seeing any enemy. Cambrai was only two miles away—and the gate to it was ours!

The tank commanders all told of shortage of petrol and ammunition; the male tanks had practically come to the end of their 200 rounds each of 6-pounder shells; the engines of the tanks were running hot because of thin oil; and the crews were exhausted. If the infantry failed to turn up, what orders should I give? I was the senior officer and in command. Tanks could attack and capture a position, but they could not hold it. I knew that we were in no condition to withstand a sudden enemy counter-attack. The problem solved itself, fortunately, with the arrival of troops about half-an-hour later. In Fontaine they found "there was no opposition, for the tanks had done their work. . . . Except for the machine gunners who had been defending the village, no fighting troops were encountered and the exits of the village were open." But, as I have said, the advancing infantry had suffered heavily, the casualties being nearly seventy per cent; "375 men in the ranks of the Seaforths had passed La Justice to the attack; now they numbered 120." The 7th Argyll and Sutherland, who reached the north end of the village, had suffered almost equally heavily. On the first anniversary of the action the 4th Seaforths marched to Fontaine-Notre-Dame, and erected there a large wooden cross in memory of those of their number who had fallen. After the War it was brought to Dingwall in Scotland, where it now stands outside the station.

At about a quarter-past five the three tanks: "Hadrian," "Havoc" and "Hong Kong," lumbering along like circus elephants, one following the other, started back. Our compasses appeared not to be reading true, so we took as a landmark a blazing object which we presumed was a tank still on fire. All went well until we got in among some trenches. In the black darkness it was difficult for the tanks to progress without danger of being ditched, so Hughes and I walked in front with flashlamps to explore the ground and pick out the best way. Coming upon a steep bank, which proved to be the side of a sunken road, we stopped the tanks and explored along the top in the hope of finding a shallow place in which to cross; suddenly shadowy figures loomed up against the white of the road; we challenged them, drawing our revolvers, to learn that they were stretcher-bearers of the 51st Division, collecting dead and wounded. They directed us to Cantaing, where we found the 4th Battalion The Gordon Highlanders in possession. I learned that their commanding officer was Lieutenant-Colonel Rowbotham, brother of the fellow I had come across at Bavincourt. He was only twenty-five! The Jocks told us with pride how he had ridden in on horseback at the head of his Battalion when they entered to take possession of the village, and how he had already won the D.S.O. and M.C. I was taken to see him; we had not met for ten years. He remarked on the day's success, saying the tanks had proved their worth. I heard later that for that particular day's work he had got a bar to his D.S.O. Going through Cantaing, "Hadrian's" petrol ran out, and a leak was discovered in the radiator; the journey was completed on the iron ration of petrol and water.

Nearing our rallying point, I met Spray walking in the direction of Fontaine. He had come out to look for us, to tell us to return, in case we had intended spending the whole night there. He took me to Pearson, who was recovering from a heart attack, in the dug-out at La Justice. I reported to him the capture of the objective.

When we parked the tanks about ten o'clock in

Orival Wood, some half-a-mile beyond La Justice, the crews were deaf from the infernal noise, and were sick when they got out into the clean, fresh air after almost eleven hours in the foul atmosphere of the tanks.

"Hermosa" turned up and reported a most eventful day. She had reached Fontaine about four o'clock—about the time we encountered the bombardment on the ridge. In front of Fontaine she had had her left-front machine-gun put out of action by a shell, and one man had been slightly wounded—the only casualty in the Section, proving the value of armour-plating in a modern battle. The gun was so smashed that it could not be replaced, having become jammed in the turret. "Hermosa" had entered the village, reconnoitred most of its streets, and had even proceeded a little way along the road to Cambrai, with the enemy retiring in front of her. In the village, on seeing a light in a house, Keay, accompanied by his corporal, entered and found that it was inhabited by French civilians; two Frenchmen in their delight embraced and kissed the corporal, while an old lady brought out her purse and offered money to Keay, who refused it, but accepted a cup of coffee instead. After patrolling the streets for about an hour, waiting for the infantry, he saw figures approaching in the darkness, and shouted "Halt! Who are you? Are you English?" "No," came the emphatic reply, "we're Scottish." They were Argyll and Sutherland Highlanders, of the 51st Division, who had entered to take over.

"Hermosa" had not left till five-fifty, but in the darkness we had missed her. Lieutenant A.

Macdonnell, R.F.A., who was Artillery Liaison Officer with the 4th Seaforths at Cambrai, said in a letter, quoted in the History of the 4th Seaforths, about this day:

*What a battle! I've seen and done so much in the last three days that I haven't time to do more than give you an outline now, which I will try and fill up with details later on. All the old "shock troops" were out on the warpath, and I was liaison to an infantry battalion (the 4th Seaforths) as it went up to attack, and thus I advanced with five different lots.*

*The old Division have done, as ever, marvellously. We advanced seven and a half miles in depth into the enemy's lines, took 30 guns and 2000 prisoners, and finished up on the evening of the 21st with a surprise attack and an impromptu show that took a village no one ever thought we would. Quite apart from that there have been the most astonishing sights—tanks advancing in lines and waves, cavalry galloping across fields with drawn swords and jumping trenches, etc. The last village we captured was intact and without a damaged roof even, and we rescued about sixty civilians. The latter were superb—fell on our necks, rushed off for secret supplies of food for us, and shouted "Vive l'Angleterre!"*

In another letter giving further details, he said:

*Early on the 21st the Huns retired (from Flesquières), and the third battalion (7th Argyll and Sutherland) went through and again I went on.*

*This time was extraordinary, as we were over the ridge and could see the whole valley and the attack coming down. Battalion Headquarters was a flag stuck in the middle of a field with a row of officers watching through field-glasses; the infantry was advancing in lines and columns and parties everywhere. Battalions in reserve were streaming up behind, and cavalry patrols were going along the ridges. We had a good deal of machine-gun fire as we went forward, but we fetched up at a farmhouse (La Justice), where we established ourselves. Reports came in very soon which made it clear that no more could be done owing to three villages in front, so the Colonel of the infantry and I went forward to see the situation. After going about 500 yards they got machine-gun and rifle fire on to us, and we lay in ruts on the road and tried to camouflage ourselves as pancakes for about twenty minutes, and then, being fed up, got up and ran like hares back again—and we were quite glad to be back again! After that we were less ambitious and stayed at Battalion Headquarters at the farm. At about half-past three we happened to glance back and saw rows of tanks advancing, so it was decided to have an impromptu attack, which was a roaring success, and captured all the villages in half an hour, the third being the ultimate objective of the Division—eight miles from the start.*

The enemy version of the attack in the Cantaing-Anneux Sector was quoted in an article in *The Royal Tank Corps Journal* of September 1936. The following is an extract from the article:

(CAMBRAI. THE SECOND DAY)

"The English artillery is bombarding Cantaing and their aeroplanes are continually diving low over the houses. Everywhere on the enemy's side movement can be seen, cavalry are at Nine Wood, and the infantry are assembling on the road Marcoing-Graincourt. It seems impossible, but we think we hear sounds of music in the middle of a great battle. The sound becomes clearer and then we realize it is the bagpipes. In Company columns the Highlanders are advancing; the commanders are mounted and can be easily identified through glasses. The English must indeed feel sure of their victory. And these beautiful targets remain unengaged. Cannot our artillery observers see them? But nothing is being done on our side. The English deploy and advance their Companies at about 700 metres; our 52nd and 232nd Regiments open rapid fire. The Company Commander telephones to the Battalion: 'It is an absolute shooting match. We are shooting standing as fast as we can.'

"The English advance stops and the numerous waves take cover.

"Small grey-black points appear here and there and continue their movements steadily forward, they are becoming larger and clearer. They must be tanks.

"Our machine-guns fire incessantly, and then rifle and grenade fire is added, but as with the Regiments of the 54th Division yesterday, so our 52nd and 232nd Regiments must admit that all efforts to stop these tanks are ineffective. We can do nothing against them. They come steadily forward and are not bound to roads or tracks. With horror we see that our wire entanglements are crushed down and that fences and even garden walls do not stop them."

The Germans give great praise to their troops who fought in Fontaine, and there is no doubt that their resistance was of a very high order. This was in part due to the fact that they were there in great strength and formed part of a good Division. It was in part also attributable to this Division having carried out special training in anti-tank measures. One feature of this training was that the forward troops should lie concealed and offer no resistance to the approaching tanks, but that when the tanks had gone past they should open fire at very short range if necessary, on the approaching infantry. If, as happened at Fontaine, there was a considerable gap between the tanks and the infantry, with no second wave of tanks available, these tactics could meet with considerable success.

It is noteworthy, however, that the tank alone was able to obtain the mastery in the open ground outside the village.

The following is an account from the German History of the fighting on the south side of the village:

"The English directed heavy fire, mixed with smoke, on the Sector of both Battalions on the 58th Regiment before he sent forward his tanks. Our artillery fire, coupled with that of our machine-guns, was unable to stop the forward movement of the tanks.

(*Above*) THE RUINS OF LA JUSTICE FARMHOUSE
When the photo was taken in 1924 the farmhouse had not been
rebuilt, but a hut was in the ruins
(*Below*) THE RIDGE BEFORE FONTAINE-NOTRE-DAME
SEEN FROM THE CHURCH
The Tanks were on this ridge when the duel between Tanks and
Artillery took place on the afternoon of the 21st November, 1917,
during the attack on Fontaine-Notre-Dame

"Their attack came chiefly against the right flank of the 2nd Battalion, and soon afterwards the tanks appeared behind the 58th.

"The front line in the whole Sector of the 58th Regiment (a Regiment equals three Battalions) was shaken. At first, individuals run back, then whole Companies, and finally this rearward movement affects the reserves. The Companies withdraw in a north-easterly direction and some of them succeed in reaching the village of Fontaine.

"This advance of the tanks from the direction of Cantaing on to Fontaine is not followed by any infantry. The 1st Battalion of the 46th Regiment about La Folie is able to see what is happening, although the English are smoking the locality.

"As soon as the Battalion Commander heard that the 58th Regiment on his right had been driven back, he placed on the west side of La Folie the 4th Company, as well as every man that could be made available from the headquarters staff."

.     .     .     .     .

The enemy report confirms that field-guns were used for anti-tank defence in the village, but that those in the open south of the village proved ineffective, as they were smothered by fire from the tanks.

The German History also contains an account of how the German infantry, whilst hiding from the tanks when they advanced, threw bundles of bombs on to them from the rear. It also gives an account of the German delight when one of the tanks' tracks was broken:

"This event was received with cheers, but we could not approach the tank, because it fired in every direction. Then suddenly a second tank appeared, which was armed with a gun and which shot straight through the wall of our house, so that we had to take flight into a yard. Nevertheless, we took up fire again, but we see, to our surprise, that the second tank has closed up on the right of the tank that we had damaged. This gives cover to the second tank and, though it is only about ten metres away, we cannot do anything. But what is happening? The second tank has taken the crew out of the first tank and goes away firing hard."

.   .   .   .   .

There was a gap in the German defences on the 21st between Fontaine and Bourlon village. The German accounts suggest that on the afternoon of the 21st opportunities for a break-through by the English existed.—(END OF EXTRACT.)

The dug-out at La Justice had been constructed by the Germans with their usual thoroughness. An excellent staircase of some twenty steps or more led down into it. Unfortunately, the entrance now faced the front line, instead of being away from it as before, when designed by the enemy for his safety. A shell well fired by the Germans might now drop right down to the bottom of the dug-out through the entrance at the top. This, in fact, did happen, but not until after we had left it.

One side of the dug-out was fitted with tiers of bunks, made of rabbit wire; while at the far end was a wooden partition, separating it from the farm cellars.

Mentally and physically exhausted, and temporarily deaf, yet with a feeling of exhilaration at the success of my tanks, I stumbled in the darkness down the steps, followed by Hardy. We found all the bunks occupied, and so we settled down to sleep on the floor. Gerrard had the bottom berth, and I stretched myself alongside it.

I learned "Hydra" had been completely disabled, its driver dying in the arms of Buckbarrow, the tank commander, who was trying to get him out.

I had had too much excitement that day, and although worn out, I could only sleep by fits and starts. I had taken off my field-boots, and once I was certain I felt a rat nibbling at my toe.

The total advance in the two days had been about seven miles, and our capture of Fontaine-Notre-Dame was the culminating point of the advance on Cambrai.

Not one of the tank officers, including myself, who reached Fontaine, had seen previous active service.

Colonel Willoughby, commanding "H" Battalion, told me that our attack and capture of Fontaine-Notre-Dame would go down into history. But it was forgotten in the excitement of the succeeding week.

Next morning (Thursday, the 22nd), G.H.Q. issued the following official communiqué, which appeared in the London newspapers of Friday, the 23rd. *"Yesterday evening our troops, moving forward north of Cantaing, attacked and captured the village of Fontaine-Notre-Dame (two miles from the Western outskirts of Cambrai), together with a number of prisoners."*

My father read of this "extremely dashing achievement" in his *Times*, without realizing that it had almost cost him his only son.

One the same day that this communiqué appeared in the newspapers, the bells of St. Paul's rang out their pæan in celebration of the Victory of Cambrai.

5

The day following our Fontaine achievement, I went down to where the tanks were parked to make certain that both machines and crews were all right.

Orival Wood, where Capt. "Ray" Macdonald and some of the fallen were buried, was an oblong strip, about 400 yards long and 250 yards wide, of saplings and undergrowth, affording fairly good cover for tanks. At the end nearest La Justice, there was an abandoned German battery, with a well-made dug-out for the gunners. The tank commanders and their crews had made themselves comfortable in it. The left gun of the battery had been knocked out by a direct hit, a proof of the amazing accuracy of our artillery. All the more wonderful, because ranges before the battle had been worked out in theory only; registering shots might have caused too much undesirable activity.

I had a sort of possessive pride in the village of Fontaine. It was with a feeling of personal loss that I heard it was no longer in our hands. "The division on the left not having succeeded in carrying Bourlon Wood, and La Folie Wood being still in the enemy's hands, Fontaine lay 'like a nut gripped between two crackers.' " That morning the enemy with fresh troops, who, in the words of the German official communiqué: *"Proved their magnificent attacking spirit in the storming of the village,"* had counter-attacked in force, and our infantry, weak and exhausted, had been unable to hold it.

When the gate to Cambrai had been ours the opportunity had not been utilized. If the cavalry had gone into the breach made by the tanks, and followed up the retreating enemy along the Fontaine-Cambrai high road, it was my opinion that Cambrai would have fallen.

Territorial gain had not been the object of the original mass tank attack. But now that fresh territory had been acquired in a degree as yet unparalleled since trench-warfare had begun, G.H.Q. were seized with an almost reckless determination not to let go their prey.

The key position of Fontaine-Notre-Dame must be regained!

Early on the morning of the 23rd (Friday), I climbed out of the stuffy dug-out to fill my lungs with fresh air. The news had reached us at La Justice that there was to be a big attack by tanks and Highlanders to recapture Fontaine. Our Company was not taking part in the attack, as it had already been in action twice, whereas other companies had been in only once. This was a respite for which I personally was truly thankful. As I stepped into the trampled patch of ground, which had once been the garden of the farmhouse, the first object that met my astonished eyes, was two Jocks having breakfast—they were seated on the dead body of a German, which was stretched out on a derelict door lying on a low box-hedge. The door, no doubt, had been used as a makeshift stretcher to bring the fatally wounded man there. I shrank from their callousness. But they seemed to be taking it all in the day's work, and were chatting to each other. Not much reverence for death, I thought!

I meditated that these hardy Highlanders were descended from fighting stock, and expected no favours of life. I remembered the Scottish father, who, when a friend tried to offer him consolation on the death of his boy in action, replied simply and unemotionally: "Yes, I have had the misfortune to lose my son!" This sort of stoicism was, I supposed, a characteristic of such a nation of warriors. It reflected the unyielding hardness of their country. I had Scottish blood in my veins through my mother's family, although on my father's side I was descended from Irish stock. Being born under "The Southern Cross," I conjectured, had knocked out of me the stoical nature of my forefathers!

I descended the staircase into the dug-out to find that on the other side of the partition a Brigade General of the Highland Division had established his H.Q. Those Jocks that I had seen upstairs were probably brigade runners. He was already in telephonic communication with the C.O.s of the infantry battalions in front of Fontaine, preparatory to the attack. Here was an opportunity to hear first-hand a General direct a battle. There and then, I decided to listen-in.

The one-sidedness of a telephone conversation is always tantalizing. One can only guess what the other person is saying. Evidently the Battalion Commanders in turn were reporting their exact positions. From time to time the General repeated the information he received to his Brigade Major. Then the barrage commenced. From inside the dug-out, it sounded muffled; but I knew from the telephone conversation that the heavies were on to the village. By the noise which came through, the bombardment was terrific. That is the end of Fontaine church, I thought!

The shells are falling short. . . . Poor blighters! Were the infantry getting them instead? The range was lengthened.

As the time for the infantry to advance on Fontaine approached, a C.O. asked: "Where are the tanks?" We in the dug-out could hear the monsters above us. They were lining up along the La Justice-Cantaing road, outside the farmhouse. Some forty of them, I was told, were going into action. As we heard the dull rumble of their tracks and exhausts fading away overhead, we knew they were off on their mission of death. The General in a clear, unexcited voice, advised a Battalion Commander that they had started. "The tanks are coming up!" he said. "They're rolling into action."

Knowing the lie of the land, I waited in tense excitement, straining my ears to hear every word of the news that filtered through. Desperately I hoped that the tanks would succeed in recapturing the village. At last word came! Some tanks are knocked out. . . . (Presumably on that memorable ridge!) . . . The village has been entered. . . . The fighting is very severe. . . . Impossible to

I

make headway. . . . Terrific machine-gun fire from roof-tops and cellars. . . . Infantry unable to follow.

I went up into the garden to take a breather. Both enemy aeroplanes and our own were humming low overhead. The crackle of machine-guns from them was in the air. Occasional shells were crashing in the field outside the garden. I was in no fire-eating mood, and sought safety again in the dug-out.

The flank of a company was exposed. . . . The General received information that the enemy was massing in La Folie Wood for a counter-attack. . . . The heavies were getting on to it now!

The tanks and the Highlanders were putting up a brave show; but, in the words of the German official communiqué, *"the enemy exhausted his forces in many fruitless assaults against the hotly-contested Fontaine and La Folie Wood."* The same German troops that on the previous day had regained the village, were now fighting in its defence *"with equal firmness and bravery."*

The fact was that the attack on Fontaine had failed.

When wounded and prisoners started to come back I went up above. I saw a handsome young German officer walking up and down the path in front of the entrance to the dug-out. He was fair and had fine, clear-cut features. It was only his grey uniform which distinguished him from being a British officer. I felt rather sorry for him. He had plenty of pride in his face. It seemed to me that he felt the disgrace of being a prisoner.

The roadway outside the farmhouse was now a

dressing-station. A large number of stretcher cases were waiting to be moved back. The form on each stretcher was covered with an army blanket. When the blanket covered the head I surmised the man was dead. I was walking on the edge of the road on the far side from the dressing-station, when I recognized Rex Davis, lying on a stretcher. His face was white. He told me that a bullet had struck him in the chest. His breathing was difficult. A tank colonel (Colonel Bryce), who was at that moment forward at La Justice, saw Davis, and realized that his lung had been pierced and that he was dying. There was only one ambulance there, and that a horse one. There was room in it for only one more stretcher. The colonel told the ambulance men that Davis must have that place. As I helped to lift the stretcher and put it in I experienced a peculiar feeling of chokiness. Though at the same time I half-envied him getting away from the bloody war. I pieced together later from various sources the complete story of what had happened. The leading tank of his section in which he was riding had developed engine trouble in front of Fontaine, and was surrounded by the enemy. In the skirmish which followed three of his gunners had been wounded. The enemy was beaten off, however, and Davis had gone on foot to another tank of his section which had been disabled, and brought back two gunners to replace the casualties in his tank. Then he started out again on foot to help another tank of his section which had been hit and put out of action. He had to go through enemy machine-gun fire, for the tank was several hundred yards in front of the foremost line of infantry. It was in the attempt to reach this tank that he was wounded. He felt a terrific thump in the chest. No one being near, he wondered momentarily who had struck him. It was only when he found it difficult to breathe, and when he coughed and blood came, that he realized it had been a bullet. He felt faint, and sank to the ground. There he lay until he saw two Germans coming towards him. With difficulty he pulled out his revolver, and covered them. They threw away their rifles, and put up their hands. He signed to them to pick him up and carry him back. In this way, he had got back behind the front line, where he was put on a stretcher and brought to the dressing-station.

As the afternoon drew to a close, the tanks—or what was left of them—returned. No progress had been made. Stories dribbled through from those who came back. They all spoke of the reckless acts of bravery on the part of the enemy. One tank commander told me how on reaching the outskirts of Fontaine the engine of his tank had stopped through a choked jet. They had been surrounded and bombed by the enemy. His gunners, three of whom were wounded, kept up Lewis gun-fire, while he worked at the carburettor. The enemy were firing at point-blank range through the gun-mountings and loop-holes of the tank, even clinging to the guns and being blown off them, calling all the time upon the crew to surrender. After three-quarters of an hour the engine was got working again, and the tank was saved from falling into the hands of the enemy. It seemed to Mustard, who was the tank commander, that the Germans had been doped: they fought so desperately.

The German official communiqué claimed that: *"Before Fontaine alone thirty tanks are lying shot to pieces, which give a picture of the forces employed by the enemy."*

At midnight the Highlanders in front of Fontaine were relieved by the Guards—the picked storm troops of the British Army. G.H.Q. was determined to possess Fontaine!

The battle raged, day in, day out, with tanks and without them, until Tuesday the 27th, when the Guards together with tanks, made a terrific assault on the village; but any ground that was gained could not be held. Philip Gibbs, writing in *The Daily Telegraph*, said of that day's fighting in Fontaine-Notre-Dame: ". . . I think no man may look into it now and live after his view—neither an English soldier nor a German soldier—because the little narrow streets which go between its burnt and broken houses are swept by bullets from our machine-guns in the south and from the enemy's in the north, and no human being could stay alive there for a second after showing himself in the village. Once there was a fountain of pure water there dedicated to Our Lady of Compassion, and French women came there to touch the foreheads of their children with a few drops of it from their finger-tips, believing in its healing virtues. Yesterday no Lady of Compassion was there to help poor suffering men. There was no compassion of any kind. Men fought in the streets and in the broken houses, and behind the walls and round the ruins of the little church of Notre Dame. To-day there are only dead bodies among the ruins and the patter of machine-gun bullets."

What a contrast to the place of six days earlier, which had looked so invitingly peaceful from the ridge as we ran the gauntlet of the German batteries, and where Keay had received coffee from a grateful old lady!

Not even the British Guards had been able to recapture and hold Fontaine!

Our minor triumph of November the 21st, before the enemy had got his second wind, had, through neglected opportunity, resulted in a battle of the first magnitude, in which the fighting had become hard, bloody and desperate; but without the victory which had been ours.

.          .          .          .          .

On the 24th we left La Justice and Orival Wood. Our first move from this forward area was to Ribécourt, where we spent the night, again in an abandoned German dug-out. Keay, who was highly strung, was by this time suffering from the reaction of his exceptionally fine performance with "Hermosa." Hughes's medical knowledge came to the rescue, and it was he who took Keay to the Casualty Clearing Station, from which he was invalided to England.

We continued our trek back, finally arriving at Fins for entrainment,

## 6

We were on our way to Winter Quarters, at Bray-sur-Somme, near Albert. Spray, as Second-in-Command and responsible for the arrangements of the Company, had gone on in advance. The male tanks already had their sponsons pushed in, preparatory to the train journey. The majority of the tanks were in need of attention—sprockets and tracks required readjustment, or probably a general overhaul and renewal of worn-out parts. During the morning of Friday, the 30th, news came through that the enemy had counter-attacked and broken through our line at two opposite points at the base of the salient, with the object of cutting off our troops in it. An S O S reached us for tanks to be rushed into action. As neither Gerrard nor Grounds had been in a second time, Pearson selected them for the attack. In Spray's absence he made me his Second-in-Command. We went round to see what tanks could be pushed in. Bown, one of Gerrard's tank commanders, was working hard at his machine, but could not get the sponsons out. They had jammed. He volunteered to take another tank in. "Hermosa" was without an officer since Keay's departure and was ready for action, since being a female tank its sponsons had not had to be pushed in for entrainment. Bown with his crew took over this tank. Seven others were comparatively ready, and were hastily got into fighting trim.

Grounds and Gerrard, each with his composite section of four tanks, were to counter-attack at Gouzeaucourt, three-and-a-half miles away, and went off at once.

Pearson and I eventually collected nineteen other tanks with which we formed a Composite Company, and started during the afternoon. We headed in the direction of Heudecourt, some two-and-three-quarter miles away, following a route south of that taken by the eight tanks that had already left. It was really late afternoon before the whole lot got away, and darkness had already fallen. About midnight Pearson and I attended a conference with the General of a dismounted Indian cavalry division. We were told their H.Q. was at a certain map reference near a "lone tree." After considerable difficulty, we located the "lone tree," in the darkness of this winter night. The conference lasted half-an-hour, during which it was decided that the attack of our nineteen tanks, supported by the dismounted Indian cavalry, should take place at dawn against Gauche Wood. We returned to the column of waiting tanks and gave them their battle-orders. Amongst these tanks were the remaining two of my section, "Hadrian" and "Havoc." The plans were so hurriedly arranged that there was no question of organizing the tanks into sections. Consequently, at dawn, they went into action against Gauche Wood, as nineteen indivdual units. It was a mere weight of metal being thrown against the Wood to crush it.

Pearson and I found ourselves on a road which the enemy began to shell. We looked around for shelter and discovered a dug-out by the roadside. We went in, but came out very quickly. It was full of bombs, electrically wired so as to blow up the road if necessary.

As the tanks started to return we went to the rallying point at Revelon Farm. There I saw one of the crew of a tank which had been blown to pieces. He had lost his reason and was running about covered with oil, and with bits of flesh, which had splashed on to him, clinging to his clothes.

The attack had been a success, and the Wood had been captured. Later, Sir Douglas Haig in his Dispatch said: ". . . a number of tanks co-operated with dismounted Indian cavalry . . . and were in a great measure responsible for the capture of the wood. Heavy fighting took place for this position, which it is clear that the enemy had decided to hold at all costs. When the infantry and cavalry finally took possession of the wood, great numbers of German dead and smashed machine-guns were found. In one spot four German machine-guns, with dead crews lying round, were discovered within a radius of twenty yards. Three German field-guns, complete with teams, were also captured in this wood."

.    .    .    .    .

At Fins I heard what had happened when the tanks under Gerrard and Grounds had attacked east of Gouzeaucourt, at the same time as we attacked Gauche Wood, on the 1st of December. All Gerrard's tanks had been disabled, three having been knocked out. The attack had proved to be "Hermosa's" last fight, and she had come to a gallant end. Bown, her voluntary commander, and four of the crew, had met their death, and the other three had been severely wounded.

Just before they started off at dawn, Bown, evidently ill at ease, had gone to Gerrard and asked him to join his tank, as he had done on the first day, November the 20th. Gerrard replied that he would willingly have gone with him but that he must go with young McCleod, who had never been in action before.

The tanks advanced against the St. Quentin Ridge. McCleod's tank, which was leading, got ditched, and in spite of repeated efforts to get it going again it could not be freed. Gerrard ordered the machine-guns and ammunition to be taken out, and formed the crew into a Lewis gun section. He took them up to a suitable place at which to form a strong-point. Having established them there, he went off towards his other three tanks. Before he reached them, he saw first one then another, then the third, receive direct hits from a·battery on the other side of the ridge, and put out of action. While he was going towards "Hermosa," eight or nine shells struck her in rapid succession; she burst into flames and soon became a roaring furnace. While at "X's" tank, one of the enemy was seen making for the top of the ridge as fast as his short legs would carry him. "X," furious at the destruction of the tanks, rushed for a machine-gun, but none was ready for firing. A 6-pounder, however, was loaded, and "X," taking accurate aim at the retreating German, fired. In Gerrard's words: "The puffing Jerry seemed suddenly to take wings, and rising gracefully into the air, disappeared over the ridge."

Gerrard formed the survivors of the tank crews into Lewis gun sections, and took them up to the strong-point he had established. Then, coming across a German machine-gun and ammunition which had been captured earlier in the day, used the gun himself against the enemy.

Across a valley, also on the St. Quentin Ridge,

he saw Grounds, and they had waved to each other.

Gerrard stayed out until only McCleod and six men remained out of the original thirty-two which had gone into action. Returning from Gouzeau-court to Fins, Gerrard and McCleod helped a Tommy who had been wounded in the foot. They put him on a bicycle which they'd found, and and wheeled him along. Suddenly, Gerrard, with his uncanny intuition, sensed a shell coming. With a yell, he pushed McCleod, the Tommy and the bicycle into the ditch, leaping in after them. Within a fraction of a second a shell crashed in the road, blowing a huge crater in the very spot where they had been. Finding that he wasn't hurt Gerrard looked round for the other two. McCleod had got a nasty gash in the neck from a fragment of the shell. The Tommy, without waiting for further assistance and forgetting all about the bicycle, was going hell-for-leather down the road.

Three of Grounds's four tanks were put out of action by direct hits. Like Gerrard, he had formed the crews into Lewis gun sections and had taken them forward to help in holding back the enemy. Having placed them to the best advantage, he had gone to get in touch with the Guards. While going along a trench he had met a party of the enemy. Making use of his previous active service experience with the infantry, he bombed them with German bombs he found in the trench. Then he brought his one remaining tank, and with the tank and a party of the Guards as bombers, succeeded in capturing about 200 yards of trench, fifteen machine-guns and numerous prisoners. The tank was in charge of a sergeant, its officer having been wounded. This N.C.O. described to me later how as his machine was about to cross a ditch he noticed a German with a machine-gun at the bottom of it. The man's eyes seemed to bulge behind his spectacles as, apparently spellbound, he waited and watched till the tank descended upon him.

.	.	.	.	.	.

We remained at Fins—I suppose in case we should be wanted again. Although it was now December, we were still under canvas, being quartered in bivouacs or bell-tents. The weather was fine, but bitterly cold. Some of us discovered that after living in German dug-outs both ourselves and our clothes had become verminous. Hughes, with his knowledge of chemistry, found a petrol sponge-down the most effective way of dealing with the trouble. Kydd, my batman, attended to my clothes, and I personally suffered no inconvenience in that direction. I remember an intimate scene at section headquarters one morning when Hardy, a pipe clamped between his jaws, and Hughes, both clad in their British warms, were seated on petrol tins solemnly investigating the inner seams of their trousers.

At Fins we had the opportunity of dealing with our correspondence. About the middle of November I had told my parents not to worry if they did not hear from me for the next few days as I was very hard worked, and assured them that I was in the best of health. At intervals during the battle I sent them *Field Service* post cards with the four words unerased: *"I am quite well."* At Ribécourt, on our trek back, I had received the first mail since the battle began. We had all sat round in a circle opening our letters, eager to know what the people at home had heard. My father, studying the newspapers, knew more about the battle of Cambrai than I did, and had taken it for granted that I was in it. Naturally he was very keen to know what part I had played. From Fins, before the German counter-attack, I replied that I was forbidden to give him inner details, and that he would have to remain satisfied with what he had gleaned from the papers. I did tell him, however, that my Section had done very well; that it had been in action twice and captured a village on the second day, and that on both occasions had come back intact. I felt rather proud of this achievement. I wrote somewhat exultantly of the splendid sensation it was to lead one's tanks into action, but added that one didn't want too much of it, and assured him that although we had come through safely it had not been an easy job.

After the counter-attack on December the 1st, I wrote saying that I had been in action again, and that although I personally had come through all right, our casualties had been very heavy—mostly wounded, fortunately. On the day I wrote this, I received from him a letter in reply to one of my *Field Service* cards in which he said it was a wonder I had survived. I entirely agreed. I forwarded to him a letter I had received from Davis, now in hospital, in which Davis had made a reference to a decoration which he expected would come my way.

With becoming modesty I advised my father not to pay too much attention to this. Although, in view of what the Colonel had said to me, and the fact that I had been made Second-in-Command of the Composite Company, I half-expected it myself. I had not been out for glory, but my father's taunt: "My son will shoulder a rifle," had not been forgotten, and it had been my ambition to prove to him that I would not break down under fire. I could now write to him with self-assurance, but I felt that a little bit of ribbon would be proof conclusive.

I had been looking forward to leave in the near future; but five days later all immediate prospect of that was cancelled. Instead we were reported to be going into Winter Quarters within a day or two. After having been in action three times within twelve days, and the Company having suffered severe casualties, my spirits began to droop. I wanted to get away from it all, and go home for a few days. I felt I had now got my remove to the Upper School. A box of eatables which my mother at this time sent me proved most acceptable.

What with bombs, shells and the bitter cold, life at Fins was not too pleasant. At dusk one afternoon, a shell burst right on one of the tents, which luckily was empty. The next tent was full of officers. The force of the explosion blew out the candles, but no one was hurt. At the time they were discussing the possibility of conducting a burial service beside "Hermosa" for Bown and the other fellows, whose ashes lay there. Gerrard, who felt Bown's death very deeply, was urging that it should be done, although the tank's position was still dangerously exposed, being in view of the enemy.

The service by the tank never took place, to Gerrard's eternal regret. For my own part I do not think that it mattered. They had been "faithful unto death," and would surely receive "a crown of life."

# CHAPTER V

# WINTER QUARTERS, NEAR ALBERT.
## CHRISTMAS 1917

### I

ON Friday, December the 7th, the Battalion made its final move to the Winter Quarters, which so far had eluded us. While the Company made the journey by train, three or four of us seized the opportunity of going by car. We motored through Peronne and across the old Somme battlefield, through Clery and Fricourt, arriving at last at Bray-sur-Somme, near Albert.

The camp, before the Germans had withdrawn to the Hindenburg Line, had been a Casualty Clearing Station for the Somme battlefield. Like Bovington, it consisted of rows of wooden huts. The hut in which I was quartered was divided up into a number of cubicles. These had probably been used as private wards. Each had its own fire, and opened on to a central corridor. I had a cubicle to myself, and was glad of a place I could call my own. Here I would be able to relax and ruminate on the recent past. I settled down to make myself comfortable. It was good to have come through it all, and find oneself in peaceful surroundings again! I experienced a feeling of exhilaration when I read through a number of letters of congratulation that awaited me. One from my father in which he predicted a decoration! I sincerely hoped that would come true! I confidently expected that certain of my officers, N.C.O.s, and men (especially Keay and his crew), would receive some reward for the Fontaine achievement, although, when I had mentioned to Pearson the names of certain fellows who had behaved splendidly (acting with coolness and good judgment, they had stuck to their posts under most trying conditions without a waver), he had remarked that they had only done their duty. More than ever I was proud of being a Captain in the Tank Corps, and part of a Company which during the last month had proved its fighting worth, and had acquitted itself with distinction.

My lucky stars seemed to shine brightly at the fall of the year! In November 1915 I had had my accident at Cambridge, it's true, but it had saved me from Gallipoli, and I'd spent Christmas at the Grand Hotel at Brighton. In December 1916 my transfer had come through to the Tank Corps; I had not been happy with the Suffolks; principally I imagine because I did not belong to the county; with the tanks I was absolutely at home, because it seemed to me that I was pulling my weight, and that my work was being appreciated. My luck had not deserted me in the November of this year. It had been more than wonderful!

The day after our arrival, Pearson and Spray had gone off on fourteen days' leave, which made me optimistic about my chances shortly after Christmas.

K

I had time now to settle down and read back numbers of *The Times* and *Daily Telegraph*, which my father had sent me. Neither of these newspapers gave any credit to the tanks for the capture of Fontaine on November the 21st. I wrote to my father mentioning that *The Times* said something to the effect that there was a "very dashing achievement by the Scotsmen" in pushing forward "the long salient into Fontaine"; but I pointed out that the War Correspondent entirely omitted "to mention that several tanks were in the village, having captured it an hour before the Scotsmen arrived—and that without the tanks they would never have been able to get into it at all." I suggested that the reason for the omission was simple—the action had taken place too far forward for any Press Correspondent to witness it.

The vivid description of the attack and capture of Fontaine-Notre-Dame on 21st November 1917, in *A History of the Fourth Battalion, The Seaforth Highlanders*, by Lieut.-Colonel M. M. Haldane (from which I have already quoted), tells a tale of valour and amazing heroism, omitted from the bald accounts given in the official communiqué and Sir Douglas Haig's Cambrai Dispatch. In addition, it gives to the tanks greater credit than was given them in these two documents. The action was thus coldly described in Haig's Cambrai Dispatch: "Late in the afternoon Fontaine-Notre-Dame was taken by troops of the 51st Division and tanks." It is clear from the Seaforths' account that, in spite of the dauntless efforts of the 51st Division, Fontaine-Notre-Dame could not have been reached, much less captured, that day without the tanks. I think it was the capture of Fontaine-Notre-Dame on 21st November which decided G.H.Q. to prolong the battle.

The evacuation of so much of the ground gained on November the 20th and 21st, and the consequent withdrawal of the line to the Flesquières Ridge, depressed me. When new ground and villages had been so gallantly captured, what a waste it all seemed to hand them back to the enemy. G.H.Q. could not have had much faith in tanks before the battle, the success of which must have exceeded their wildest dreams. Otherwise how could one explain that there were no fresh troops to relieve the Highlanders at Fontaine on November the 21st? They were physically exhausted men who had to withstand the fierce German attack of the following morning.

The truth was that there had not been sufficient troops available to make use of the opportunity which the tanks had created. The recapture of Fontaine by the enemy was the turning point of the battle. My father blamed me for having gone too far forward on November the 21st, and captured Fontaine without orders. He could see no other explanation. If G.H.Q. had really wanted Fontaine, he argued, and ordered us to attack and capture it, why were there not more troops to follow up our success? I disillusioned him! He was eloquent, too, over the disaster of November the 30th, when the Germans had made their successful counter-offensive! Why was the line so thinly garrisoned? And he was eager to know all I could tell him of my third action. My replies were cautious, for there was a Censor. I merely told him that I had gone into action as Second-in-Command of a Composite Company from the Brigade.

About ten days after our arrival at Bray, the Brigadier chanced to see me, and I experienced a thrill when he personally congratulated me on our success in the second day's action. My enthusiasm for the tanks reached its summit, and I even thought that I might make the Army a career. But in reality the glories of War did not appeal to me. I reflected that it was not until after the job was done that you realized how successful you had been, and how much depended on the issue.

The weather entered into the spirit of the season. Snow fell and lay a foot deep on the ground. To prevent the cylinders being cracked by frost, the tank engines had to be started up at intervals, and special guards were detailed for this job. The sharp cold made fires essential. No coal was issued to us, and we had to rely on timber salvaged from derelict dug-outs to keep the stoves going. There was difficulty in obtaining such fuel, for it was getting scarce. Everybody was out on the scrounge, endeavouring to collect as much as possible before it was all gone. Kydd, with admirable foresight, kept a sufficient reserve so that my cubicle was never cold.

There was a wood fatigue, various parties going out to collect what they could. These parties made unauthorized use of a light-railway near the camp. An empty bogie was pushed up to the place where they collected the wood. Having loaded the timber on to the bogie, the men clambered on top and made the most of a free ride home down the slope. Once, however, some Royal Engineers were using the line, driving a small motor up the incline. There were shouts of warning, but the collision was inevitable as there was no means of stopping the bogie. The men managed to jump clear before the crash occurred. Fortunately nobody was injured; but the R.E.s were roused by it to a frenzy of eloquence.

The ruined town of Albert was just about an hour's walk from the camp, and we made frequent excursions there to get a glimpse of civilian life. Numbers of the population had already returned and shops had been reopened. We made numerous purchases in preparation for Christmas. One of the most popular commodities was Camembert cheese. The Grand Restaurant, near the station, was popular on account of its appetizing lunches and dinners. The "patron" was also the *chef*, and his three pretty daughters attended the tables. They were capable, with typical French shrewdness, and permitted no familiarities. One of them was called Germaine. Gerrard jokingly said she was a little German, and called her Bochette. Her knowledge of English being evidently limited, and as the French equivalent *Allemande* was totally dissimilar, the play upon her name was lost upon her. She was furiously indignant, and stamping her foot, exclaimed that she had been insulted. I murmured: "You've put your foot in it, old man!" Gerrard, however, assumed an expression of surprised innocence, and by diverting her attention, made his peace.

An excursion to Amiens, which at this time was a civilian town in all its glory, meant a twenty-mile journey by car. To do Christmas shopping we had the opportunity to go there once or twice. The Hôtel du Rhin was patronized for luncheon; but before that we became acquainted with Aux Huitres and Charley's Bar in the *rue Corps Nu sans Teste.* Hardy was horrified at this seemingly unblushing example of Gallic frankness. His imperfect knowledge of archaic French translated it as "the street of the nude castrated body." Glanville (the Company Mess President) was a *connoisseur* in the matter of food, wine and cigars, and took charge of the luncheon arrangements. Then it was I received my introduction to a "magnum" of champagne.

The Tank Corps Christmas Card seemed to typify the spirit of the moment. The picture was of two tanks—one in the foreground and one in the background. There was a Tommy looking out of the top manhole of both, each waving to the other across an expanse of snow. The obvious greeting was, "Cheerio," although the words were: "Christmas Greetings 1917. All best wishes." Since the 15th of September 1916, when the first tanks had participated in the battle of the Somme, tanks had taken part in the battles of the Ancre, Arras, Messines, 3rd Ypres and Cambrai, and these were proudly remembered on the card.

On the 3rd of January 1918, an inquiry came through from Brigade for general statistics and records of the recent actions. Three days later I sent in the following report:

*"To: O.C. 23 Coy., H Bn.,*
  *Tank Corps,*
    *January 6th, 1918.*

*With reference to inquiry of 3/1/18, I have the honour to submit the following:*

*During the recent actions No. 7 section, 23 Company, was engaged in the fighting in or around four villages:*
  *On the 20th RIBÉCOURT and MARCOING.*
  *On the 21st CANTAING and FONTAINE.*
*This Section, together with one other tank, captured the village of FONTAINE on the 21st.*

*Numerous prisoners were taken on the 20th, and handed to infantry after a battery of machine-guns had been destroyed near MARCOING.*

*On the 21st a trench-mortar battery and three field-guns were silenced in the neighbourhood of CANTAING MILL and FONTAINE respectively.*

*The three tanks of this section rallied after each action without injury to tanks, or casualty amongst personnel, after having been in action for eight hours on the 20th and eleven hours on the 21st.*

*This, I think, constitutes a record of work accomplished by a section without loss of life or material.*

*D. E. HICKEY (Capt.),*
  *O.C. No. 7 Section,*
    *23 Coy.*

This report should have been qualified, perhaps, to the extent that in front of Fontaine, "Hermosa" had a Lewis gun put out of action, and one man had been slightly wounded. But, I suppose,

at the time of writing the report I thought that such
"loss of . . . material" or "casualty amongst personnel" was insignificant.

As far as I remember, Pearson did not seem to
think this report of much importance.

Next day, the list of awards for our Battalion
was pinned up on the notice-board in the ante-room.
It was not a long one—some fourteen names of
officers, in addition to those of other ranks. With
a sensation similar to that of scanning examination
results, I glanced rapidly down the names. Pratt,
Pearson, Grounds and Gerrard—they had each got
a D.S.O.! Four D.S.O.s for the Battalion, and
three of them for our Company! For two section
commanders to receive an order which was usually
only conferred on senior officers, was a signal
honour. Among the M.C.s were Glanville, Davis
and Mustard. These were all immediate awards
for gallantry in the field. Again I went through
the list. I realized that not one of my Section was
mentioned in it. I turned away, experiencing a
sense of frustration and helplessness. In the solitude of my cubicle I tried to reason the matter out,
and to push away the feeling of injustice which
began to possess me. But I kept my feelings to
myself, and gave no sign of my disappointment.

The repression of my feelings began to have its
effect on me. Up to then I had been perfectly
healthy and happy with the tanks. Now, however,
I could not sleep and began to suffer an acute
physical pain.

One night was so bitterly cold and wet that I
determined to make myself really comfortable in
my cubicle. I stoked up my fire to capacity; got

into pyjamas, and stretched myself on the camp-bed. The heat made me drowsy and I fell into an uneasy sleep. Something seemed to be troubling me, and I could not make out what it was. Then I seemed to be watching a fire from which heavy fumes were pouring forth. In my dream I could not do anything to get away, although I was being stifled. I had almost got to the stage of choking, when with a tremendous effort I regained my breath. Then I woke with a start, and found my cubicle full of suffocating smoke. I jumped out of bed. Part of the fire had fallen from the stove on to the wooden floor beyond the metal sheet on which the stove was placed. The wood was smouldering badly. Actually a hole had already been burnt right through the floor. I threw water over it, and damped the whole fire down.

Another incident connected with fire, had to do with one of the newcomers. I was passing one of the cubicles after lunch one day, when I was startled by a tremendous flash and explosion, followed by a scream. I burst into the cubicle to find that a subaltern, not satisfied with the warmth given out by his fire, had poured petrol direct from the tin on to it, to liven it up. The result exceeded his expectations! I was amazed to find he was only slightly singed.

.        .        .        .        .

Buckbarrow, the commander of the ill-fated "Hydra," which had been knocked out on the 21st November, had been given the same leave as myself. We made the journey together, setting off on the afternoon before our leave was due to commence.  We reached Boulogne that night and put up at an Officers' rest-house there.

.    .    .    .    .

It was the afternoon of Saturday, the 16th, before I arrived back at Bray.  For some reason or other the return journey took twenty-four hours longer.  We had about four days' notice to prepare for another move.  After a stay of eleven weeks, we departed on Friday, the 22nd of February.

CHAPTER VI

# THE MARCH RETREAT. AT THE GAP. FIGHTING A REAR-GUARD ACTION ACROSS THE OLD SOMME BATTLEFIELD

I

WE were once more in the battle zone, again in the Bapaume-Cambrai neighbourhood. Our quarters were in Nissen huts situated at regular intervals along the half-mile of sunken road connecting the village of Bertincourt with Vélu Wood, where our tanks were concealed. The road ran roughly parallel with our front line and some three or four miles behind it.

In appearance a Nissen hut was like a half-section of a large steamer funnel sliced down from top to bottom and placed tunnel-wise on the ground. It was made entirely of galvanized iron, except for the ends, which were boarded up. The front had a door in addition to the two cloth-covered windows which let in a fair amount of light but kept out the wind and rain. Compared with a tent or dug-out, the hut was much more comfort-able, but gave no protection from shells or bombs. An empty Nissen hut was one of the most cheerless desolate things one can imagine, but it assumed an almost homely atmosphere when a few personal belongings were strewn about. We used the tanks to bring up our kit, and made our quarters comfortable with collapsible furniture. The hut was warmed by an abominably smoky wood stove. The door was latchless, and had to be wedged to keep it shut. But in spite of these minor disadvantages, and the bitterly cold weather with occasional hail showers, we managed to obtain a certain amount of warmth.

The tanks had been brought up to this forward position in preparation for the big German attack which had been talked of for so long. Rumours of it had been in the air as far back as the beginning of February when I was on leave. It was expected that the enemy would make some desperate attempt to break through in view of the extravagant promises which had been made to the German people. But where or when the much advertised offensive would take place none of us knew.

Each morning in the eerie, expectant light which precedes dawn, our company "stood-to" with the rest of the battalion, two deep in the sunken road, ready for the enemy attack, if it should come. At this unearthly hour of four in the morning, I envied Gerrard his ability to shave and dress at high speed. He could always reckon on ten minutes longer in bed.

Vélu Wood was an oblong strip about half-a-mile deep, tapering towards Bertincourt. It was thick enough to conceal the tanks effectually at its narrow end. At one time it had been part of the estate of a château, situated on the far side, adjoining the village of Vélu, but now deserted. Near the château, a big naval gun, mounted on a railway truck, had been run in on a siding from the main railway line. Its shells were the size of a small barrel, and it was reported to fire into Cambrai, twelve miles away. Each time the gun fired the surrounding neighbourhood shook. One night some A.S.C. men, unaware of the presence of the gun, bivouacked in the wood. Having seen to their horses, they settled down to a game of cards by candlelight. Without any warning the gun fired. The vibration was so tremendous, the candles were blown out, and the horses, terrified by the noise, stampeded.

During the day the men worked on the tanks, oiling, greasing, adjusting, polishing, having everything in perfect working order ready to start at a few minutes' notice. The officers spent the hours of daylight exploring and reconnoitring the lie of the land until they knew it inside out. For every conceivable form of attack in our sector, an immediate counter-attack was planned and rehearsed. Everyone knew exactly what his job was in each and every eventuality. We found that supply and ammunition dumps had been formed. Lines of trenches, protected by barbed wire, had been dug and fortified behind the front line, making use of the lie of the land, in what was called the "battle zone." In view of all these preparations, it seemed to me impossible that the Boche, if he attacked, could make any definite advance, beyond a few minor local successes.

Two of the schemes of counter-attack on which we spent a good deal of time were against Doignies and against Hermies, about one or two miles from the firing line. If the enemy captured either of these places, we knew chapter and verse what to do. From Doignies it was possible to see Fontaine-Notre-Dame, seven miles away, along the Bapaume-Cambrai road, for we were now behind the Flesquières salient, to which the line had been withdrawn after the battle of Cambrai. Ytres, our old railhead for Cambrai, was only about a mile south of Bertincourt.

Of my original Section of tanks, I still had "Hadrian" and "Havoc," "Hermosa" being replaced by "No. 29." Tanks now were to be known only by numbers; but "Nos. 27 and 28," were still "Havoc" and Hadrian" to me. Hughes became a Tank Instructor and Hardy, the last of my Cambrai tank commanders, now became Company Workshop Officer, replacing Merrell. Mickle, one of the original Company, was in charge of "Havoc" (No. 27), while "Hadrian" (No. 28) and "No. 29," were under the command of two newcomers, Miles and Beddard respectively.

Of all the parts of the front I had been in, nowhere had I found better provision for our comfort and entertainment. At Bertincourt there was a Divisional Cinema, and two pierrot troupes— "The Gaspers," and "The Duds"—the former run by Morris Harvey of the Pelissier "Follies." Here, too, it was possible to obtain the luxury of a hot bath. There was, in addition, an officers' club, consisting of a single room built with the help of a few sheets of galvanized iron in the débris of a shattered house. It was furnished with comfortable chairs, where one could lounge at ease in the evening, smoke a pipe, read the daily and weekly papers, and sip a final nightcap—whisky-and-soda, or Bass. In this connection, somebody quoted from *King Henry V* : "And gentlemen in England now abed shall think themselves accursed, they were not here." It was rather appropriate in view of the heartache some people at home seemed to suffer because of the abstemiousness forced upon them.

Day followed day, and week followed week, until we had been nearly a month at Vélu. We had a spell of glorious weather. Though the nights were cold, the days were warm, and the country was bathed in sunlight. The air was filled with the fragrance and exhilaration of spring. Sitting at the door of my Nissen hut, I gazed out across an open, undulating countryside, clothed in tender green, with here and there copses bursting into life, after the long winter. I could almost imagine that it was Hampstead Heath spreading out before me. In spite of the surrounding rustic charm, I felt that the warm, sunny days were wasted, and I wished I were at the seaside. I longed too for a glimpse of civilization, which had been missing since my London leave. Each night we were reminded of the purpose of our presence in this comparatively undisturbed spot, by the crash of bombs, and the whizz of shells passing overhead. The days spent in the open air made me feel so tired and sleepy that even these uncomfortable reminders of war did not keep me awake. I could have enjoyed these pleasant days had it not been for the existing feeling of tension. Any moment this relatively peaceful existence might come to a sudden end. When at night the enemy guns became uncommonly active, we wondered if they heralded for the early hours the much-vaunted offensive. But

as the days slipped by without any unusual indications, it seemed to me unlikely that the Boche
would attack for some time yet. I wrote home
to this effect on the 19th! But I wished that if
he was going to attack, he would hurry up
about it.

By now I had been issued with my "Officer's
Record of Services. Army Book 439," which I
handed over to my C.O. for his signature and
remarks, if any. There were none. As far as my
active service with the B.E.F. was concerned, I
might not have done anything.

On the 19th the weather suddenly changed. A
semi-tropical thunderstorm broke over our sector.
The air seemed to be electrically charged.

## 2

On Thursday, the 21st of March, "stand-to" was
at four-thirty in the morning. It was still quite
dark, and there was a thick, heavy mist. We had
been shivering in the cold for some time when a
few enemy guns began to boom. Instantly the
whole battle-front seemed to join in, and a short
but intense bombardment followed. Instead of
returning to the huts at five o'clock we continued
to "stand-to." We could see nothing for the mist,
and the news that dribbled through was contra-
dictory. That the enemy had attacked, and broken
through in places, was certain. We expected any
moment to get orders to man the tanks, and
counter-attack immediately according to one of the
prearranged plans. But minutes lengthened into
hours. We did not know whether the enemy was

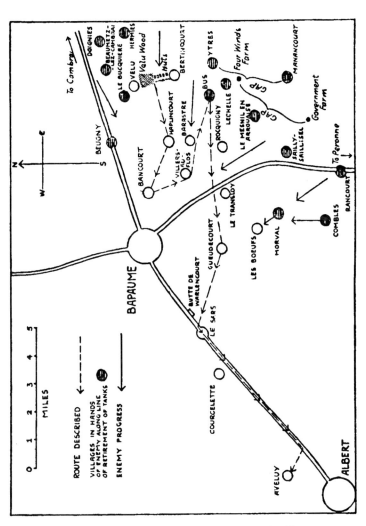

MARCH RETREAT I. "AT THE GAP"

L

advancing upon us or whether he was held. The mist was still so thick we could not see farther than thirty to forty yards. Shells screamed through the air over us. A few deafening crashes near at hand told us that the enemy had the range of our road and Nissen huts. No serious damage appeared to have been done. I had that horrible feeling which develops in the pit of the stomach on such occasions. We continued to wait, and still no orders came.

Midday came and went. The mist instead of lifting clung to the ground. I suppose we ate, but I have no recollection of it. I remember hearing that the enemy had got Doignies. He must now be only two miles away from the tanks, which were still in the wood. It would take time to get them out from among the trees, and the Boche might easily be upon us before we could get them into the open. It was reported that he was being held in the "battle zone," along a line somewhere between Doignies and Hermies. We knew exactly what to do, but had to wait for orders to do it.

As the afternoon drew to its close the mist thickened. Then orders came. A composite company consisting of two sections from our Company and two from Major Blackburn's, was to counter-attack under him, against Doignies and Hermies. The two sections from our Company detailed for the job were No. 5, Thorburn's, and No. 6, Gerrard's. I have a recollection of Gerrard's back as he hurried along the sunken road towards Vélu Wood to collect his tanks. Sections 7 and 8, mine and Edwards', were to take their tanks from the wood and go to Haplincourt, about two miles back.

We were to leave everything in the huts. Our kit would be taken back by motor lorry.

The wood was being shelled as the tanks left. As they banged and clattered along one after the other ingloriously away from the enemy, shells were falling on either side of the route they were taking, and an unusual puff of smoke hung in the air where some of the shells burst. I began to notice a peculiar smell mingling with that of the exhaust of the tanks. It was not unpleasant—rather like burnt sugar! I suspected that it was "gas," and I passed the word along to put on box-respirators. It proved to be mustard gas. Dusk had fallen when we reached our destination and found shelter for ourselves and our tanks under the roof of an open hay-shed. My throat was aching and my voice husky—the result of "gas."

This was the first stage of our retreat. Next morning I saw the tank, "Hong Kong," which had come back during the night from the counter-attack. This was the one tank, in addition to the three of my Section, which had reached Fontaine on the 21st of November. It looked like hammered, burnished pewter, and was perforated in many places by bullets. Viveash, still its commander, told me that the fire of the enemy machine-guns against it at close quarters had been intense. When bullets had pierced the armour-plating they had ricocheted inside the tank until their force was spent. The impact of bullets at close range striking the outside made a kind of fireworks inside the tank, as particles of metal of the armour-plating flew off. If one was not careful, these small bits of metal got into the eyes and skin. Before

Cambrai, a metal visor with chain armour had been issued as a protection against "splash." That was the technical name for these "fireworks." But the visor was not much used, because one could see so little through it. Viveash explained to me that the belated counter-attack had been unsuccessful, for in the enshrouding mist and darkness it had been practically impossible to see the enemy although they had been right in among him. It was a disappointment that, after a month's preparations, and after we had been on the alert the whole day, none of our prearranged plans had been carried through until it was too late, and conditions made their success impossible.

The 22nd was a clear day, and as the village of Haplincourt lay high, we had an excellent panoramic view of the country between us and the still invisible enemy. Late in the afternoon I watched the big naval gun make its escape from Vélu Wood. Enemy shells were falling on both sides of the line, as a full-size locomotive slowly hauled the monster with its trucks away. In the distance it looked like a toy train. About the same time I could see a number of tanks coming back from an attack. They were two or three miles away, and looked like large slugs, scurrying to safety, chased by puffs of smoke.

Next day, the 23rd, the enemy had advanced beyond Vélu village, capturing two villages just to the north of us. In front of us the line was being held at our Nissen huts, between Vélu Wood and Bertincourt. Ytres, to which the right wing of the Third Army had been forced to withdraw owing to the falling back of the Fifth Army further south, was only three miles from Haplincourt, and south of us. Sir Douglas Haig, in his Dispatch, said: *"At the junction of the Third and Fifth Armies the situation . . . as the day wore on . . . became critical."* The flanks of the two Armies lost touch, resulting in a gap of about three miles. At Ytres approximately, the right flank of the Third Army, to which we belonged, was in the air. To resume quoting Sir Douglas Haig's Dispatch, *"Though vigorous efforts were made to re-establish touch both by the 47th Division, under the command of Major-General Sir G. F. Gorringe, K.C.B., K.C.M.G., D.S.O., and by a brigade of the 2nd Division, Major-General C. E. Pereira, C.B., C.M.G., commanding the division, they were unsuccessful. . . . At dusk . . . the line was still in movement. Small parties of the enemy searched constantly for gaps, and, having found them, bodies of German infantry pressed through in force and compelled our troops to make further withdrawals."*

We were ordered to move two miles farther back, and spent that night at Bancourt.

## 3

*"During the night of 23rd-24th March the situation on the battle front remained unchanged as far south as the neighbourhood of Ytres. Beyond that point divisions and brigades had lost touch in the course of their frequent withdrawals, and under the constant pressure of the enemy the rearward movement continued. At dawn German infantry had already reached Bus, Lechelle, and Le Mesnil-en-Arrouaise . . . It became necessary to order the*

*evacuation of Bertincourt, and gradually to swing
back the right of the Third Army in conformity
with the movement farther south."* So ran Sir
Douglas Haig's Dispatch.

During the early part of the 24th—Palm Sunday
—the enemy continued to advance, and captured
further villages to the south.

At eleven o'clock in the morning I received
orders from Grounds, now Company Commander,
for my three tanks to go into action at Bus, to
"demonstrate" (that was the word used) in front of
the village, and thus distract the enemy's attention
from Bertincourt, so that the infantry there might
extricate themselves from their threatened isolation
in it.  Bus was about a mile south and slightly
west of Bertincourt.  After the action the tanks
were to rally at Gueudecourt, five miles or so back,
due west from Bus.  My Section was near the head
of the column of some twenty tanks which started
off.  We followed a southerly route, past the
western outskirts of Villers-au-Flos, and then
easterly to the southern edge of Barastre.  Between
these two villages, "Hadrian" (No. 28) and "No.
29," developed mechanical trouble, and were compelled to stop for repairs.  With "Havoc" (No. 27),
I pushed on towards Bus.

About noon, when at the southern outskirts of
Barastre, near Crucifix Corner, I joined forces with
MacFarlane, a Second-Lieutenant of Blackburn's
company; he was acting section commander and
his tanks were under the same orders as mine.
Once again I was the senior officer on the spot.

An enormous green field lay between us and
the village of Bus, which seemed to rise out of the

hedge at the far end. The atmosphere was clear
and there were frequent bursts of sunshine. The
ground was hard and ideal for tanks. As they
charged forward at "top" speed against the village
with 6-pounder and machine-guns blazing, I was
reminded of the charge of the tanks at Fontaine on
the 21st of November. MacFarlane and I followed
on foot, to keep in touch with the situation. These
tanks formed the extreme end of the right flank
of the Third Army, and there was nothing between
us and the Fifth Army, retreating some four miles
away. We were, in fact, at the gap! As the tanks
approached Bus, four or five men in khaki rushed
out of the village with their hands up, towards the
machines. MacFarlane and I began to wonder
(and so did the tank commanders, as I heard later),
if a mistake had been made, and the tanks were
firing into a village held by our troops. We hurried
to meet two of them who were now coming back
towards us. They were very badly shaken, and
told us they were infantrymen who had been captured by the enemy earlier in the day, and had
been kept prisoners in the village. As the tanks
had charged it, the Germans had fled, leaving them
to regain their liberty. They stated that German
cavalry had been in the vicinity of Bus, but had
left on seeing the tanks.

To the right on a ridge about a mile away, I saw
several figures—one on horseback—as though
observing the situation. Then machine-guns began
to crackle on the left—from the east side of
Barastre. MacFarlane glanced round with a sniff,
and remarked: "They have got in up there!" It
was not until much later that I learned that four

attacks had been beaten off Barastre that morning.

At this moment MacFarlane noticed that one of his tanks had stopped, apparently out of action. He left me to go and investigate. Having learnt from the two escaped prisoners that Bus was clear of the enemy, and seeing that his artillery was becoming active, I hastened towards the village to rally the tanks. No one feels courageous all the time; but just then I was in a fearless mood; the thought at the back of my mind was, "Well, this time I shall win something." I went on swinging my leaded cane by its leather thong. On the way, I met a third man, who had also escaped, and he told me the same story as the others. Heavy machine-gun fire was now coming from Barastre, and bullets were flying about. It crossed my mind that I was doing no more than these other fellows were. A fourth man was coming to meet me, when he was shot through the head and fell in a shell-hole. I woke up then! I went to see if I could do anything; but he was dead. A few minutes later I got inside my tank (dear old "Havoc!") which with the others was returning. The crew seemed to be as pleased to see me as I was to see them. The stuffy, steel box was a haven of refuge. The gunners of "Havoc" had blazed away at Bus until there were no more shells to blaze with.

After we had got clear of the field, I saw the infantry retiring in extended order, as calmly as though they were carrying out practice manœuvres. They had got away from Bertincourt according to plan. In this connection, Major-General C. E. Pereira, commanding the 2nd Division, wrote to the Commander of the V Corps:

*2nd Division, 1st April 1918.*

*V Corps.*

 *I wish to bring to your notice the invaluable assistance given to the 2nd Division by the 8th Battalion Tank Corps, when the division had great difficulty in extricating itself from the Green Line owing to the exposed flanks.*

 *There is no doubt that the whole-hearted support of the 8th Battalion saved us many casualties, and the 2nd Division are very grateful for their help.*

*C. E. PEREIRA, Major-General,*
*Commanding 2nd Division.*

 Since Cambrai the nomenclature of tank battalions had changed, and "H" Battalion was now the "8th".

  .  .  .  .  .

 Our route to the rallying-point at Gueudecourt lay (as I have said) due west, and it crossed the Bapaume-Peronne road at the Sugar Factory, just north of Le Transloy. As we approached this part of the old Somme battlefield things seemed to be humming, and there was a considerable amount of activity. Not only were men moving in a westerly direction (like myself) presumably from Bertincourt, but there were troops coming up from the south. All around there was an orderly confusion. My speculations as to what was happening down there were cut short by an enemy aeroplane swooping down over my one remaining tank. I was walking outside and immediately flung myself in a shell-hole, hoping to escape unnoticed. The plane machine-gunned the tank, perforating the silencer on top. It was so low I could see the pilot, and half drew my revolver, with the intention of having a shot at him, as he flew over me. But discretion prevailed. I realized that with a revolver the chances were I should miss him, but the attempt would probably infuriate him, and like an attacked wasp he would concentrate on me with undesirable consequences.

The enemy was in reality pressing northwards towards Bapaume, through the gap. Rocquigny, a mile south of Barastre, had been held until well into the afternoon, its defenders, as Sir Douglas Haig said in his Dispatch: *"beating off all attacks with rifle and machine-gun fire, until the enemy worked round their flank between Rocquigny and Le Transloy and forced them to withdraw."*

"Hadrian" (No. 28) and "No. 29," unable to get going, found that the infantry retiring from Bertincourt had passed, leaving them to face the enemy. Lewis guns and ammunition had been removed from the tanks, and the crews had formed strongpoints between Villers-au-Flos and Barastre. There they had helped to hold up the enemy's advance, and not until the last moment had they poured petrol over the tanks, and set fire to them.

Hardy and Spray on their own, fired a Lewis-gun in a strong-point they established, until the enemy was quite close. Hardy was the possessor of a fur lining to his British warm. It had originally belonged to his grandmother, and he had the conviction that while he wore it, in some way the old lady's spirit protected him. Whether he

was wearing the amulet or not, at this time, I do
not know, but he got away unscathed.

In many cases tanks were knocked out by the
enemy artillery.

"Hong Kong" was one of the tanks which went
into action that day at Barastre. In Dessart Wood,
just before the battle of Cambrai, in some inexplic-
able way, a horseshoe had become attached to the
tank. It hung insecurely from a bolt, and in spite
of all the joltings and shakings the tank received,
the horseshoe remained in its place. Viveash had
taken this tank into action four times: Cambrai,
the 20th November; Fontaine, the 21st November;
Gauche Wood, the 1st December, and Doignies,
the 21st March. And always without mishap!
Just before he started out with her on this fifth
action, the horseshoe fell off. At Crucifix Corner,
Barastre, the gallant "Hong Kong" met her
end, receiving a direct hit. Four of the crew
were wounded, though Viveash himself escaped
uninjured.

After an exciting trek, we reached Gueudecourt.
There Major Pratt, who was now second-in-command of the Battalion, told me to go with my
solitary tank four miles further back to Courcelette,
on the Bapaume-Albert road. The enemy, having
crossed the Bapaume-Peronne road, were advancing on Les Boeufs, in a northerly direction, only a
mile away, and right across our westerly line of
retreat. To quote again Sir Douglas Haig: *"Their
continued progress threatened to sever the con-
nexion between the Fifth and Third Armies and the
situation was serious. . . . The withdrawal of the
right and centre of the Third Army was carried out*

*during the afternoon and evening in circumstances of great difficulty, as on the right flank bodies of German infantry were already between our troops and the positions to which they were directed to fall back."*

Referring to these actions, *The Daily Graphic* stated: "Between Barastre and Les Boeufs, not far from where the first tanks appeared in war on the 15th September 1916, a number of tanks fought a slow and deliberate rearguard action last Sunday, and the survivors, despite numerous attempts to capture them with their crews, returned." *The Time* War Correspondent wrote: "On the 24th the tanks did brilliant rearguard fighting in the area of Barastre and Les Boeufs, holding the enemy in check as he came on, and slowly withdrawing with a sting in their tails . . ."

We were now crossing the old Somme battle-field. The country was scarred and torn, trees were stripped bare, and villages were heaps of ruins. Whatever orderliness there had been in the retreat up to now, seemed to disappear. To the eye, the British Army was groups of men wandering back on their own, worn out, disorganized, and utterly bewildered as to what was going to happen next. With other tanks, all suffering from some defect, I trekked along. I met Colonel Willoughby with his R.S.M. He stopped and spoke to me. We agreed that the outlook was very black, and expected peace within the next three or four days. It seemed to me that the end of the British Empire was in sight. The situation seemed hopeless. Here and there a machine-gun crackled away in a despairing attempt to delay the advance. As we went along my thirst became unbearable. I had drunk my water-bottle dry and expressed my thoughts aloud. Someone handed me a bottle of "Bass!" It came from the rear of one of the tanks, where there was a whole crate. I was told it had been salvaged *en route*.

Instead of arriving at Courcelette, we struck the Bapaume-Albert road between the Butte de Warlencourt and Le Sars. Here in a deserted hut I found a blanket, which I commandeered. I passed a little group of three or four Tommies on the roadside. They were supporting a comrade who had been wounded. The man was stripped to the waist, and swaying on his feet. His face was ashen, and he gasped for breath, as his companions tried in vain to staunch the bullet-hole in his chest, from which his life-blood was streaming. "A Christ of the Battlefields!" The words leapt unbidden to my mind. They and that scene became an undying memory. He epitomized for me the agony of the War. Those who made the supreme sacrifice gave their life that others might live. I wondered how men endured such suffering and hardship with so much patience and cheerfulness, and what were they likely to win from it all.

I trudged along the road, the tanks keeping to the left side.

Twilight was rapidly falling.

It was easier walking now, but I was dead beat. It had been a tedious business getting the tanks back across the shell-holes of the old battlefield. There was a shortage of petrol and water, and where either of these failed, that tank was supplied from another which still had a fairly good supply.

We reached Courcelette at last, in the dusk, and hoped to rest. There was a muster of the survivors of the Battalion, and I fell in again with Gerrard whom I had not seen since the afternoon of the 21st of March. The Lewis guns and S.A. ammunition were taken out of the tanks, which were left with skeleton crews with the object, I thought, of getting them back as best they could. Then we got orders to withdraw further, and wearily we started off again. I learned later that instead the tanks were sacrificed to the gods of Necessity. They were bathed in their own petrol, and set alight. Hardy told me that this task, allotted to him as Workshops Officer, had almost broken his heart. It was like killing off a faithful companion.

Marching back along the Bapaume-Albert road, the men were burdened with the Lewis guns and S.A. ammunition, both in drums and boxes, taken from the tanks. It was impossible to keep route march formation. Everybody struggled along as best he could. We discovered the guns and ammunition were diminishing in number. Evidently they were falling by the way. We halted every now and again to count them, but in the darkness it was difficult to make an effective check, and the men were too tired to care much what happened.

As we tramped along Gerrard told me his story, of which Glanville, years later, gave me further details over a lobster mayonnaise at the National Liberal Club. Piecing the two together, with what Viveash had already told me, this is what had happened. On the evening of the 21st of March, between six o'clock and half-past, the composite company of twelve tanks had gone into action. On reaching the ridge in front of Doignies, Gerrard had found that the infantry holding the line had no orders to counter-attack, and so his tanks had gone into action without any support. Glanville's experience was more or less the same as Viveash's. Owing to the ground mist and darkness, it was impossible to see where they were. They knew they were right in among the Germans, because of the intense machine-gun fire at close range, yet they could not see them. Glanville decided to tackle the situation by driving his tank directly against the bullets in the hope of crushing the machine-guns responsible. But all to no purpose! They could not even see the flashes of the machine-guns. Then Glanville found himself in a real difficulty. Manœuvring his tank in this way in the mist and darkness which enveloped him, he had completely lost his bearings. The compass, upset by the firing, was not reading true, and the blackness outside prevented him picking out any landmark. Bullets had pierced the tank, and he and most of the crew had been wounded (some seriously, some slightly) either by them, or by "splash." In a quandary, and trying to think out the best course of action, he repeated subconsciously aloud, "What shall I do? What shall I do?" One of the crew in a state of panic, said, "Surrender, sir! Surrender!" Glanville told him brusquely to shut up. His immediate fear was that the tank would be bombed, and definitely put out of action, and he ordered the crew to keep a sharp look-out for anyone approaching too close to the tank. Time stood still. He got out in an attempt to find his bearings, but it was no use. Getting in again, he told the crew that they must wait until the moon came out, and by its position he would know which way to steer. About fifteen minutes' suspense followed. Then the moon did come out. He took a bearing by it, and the tank started to move back. After some little distance, figures were outlined at about a hundred yards, or less. The crew were at once eager to fire at them, but Glanville stopped them, saying they might be our own troops. In point of fact, they were. It was the very Company that Gerrard had finally persuaded to follow him, although they were already badly cut up. After a good deal of debate, the attack was washed out, owing to the impossibility of locating the enemy, and the danger of the tanks firing into our own troops. The tanks, or what was left of them, went back to rally at the Quarry—really nothing more than a sunken road. Viveash, who really belonged to Thorburn's Section attacking to the right, between Doignies and Hermies, had lost his bearings, too, and had rallied under Gerrard. I presume that Viveash made his way back independently to Haplincourt, and that was how I saw him there. As Thorburn failed to turn up at the Quarry, Gerrard received Major Blackburn's permission to go and look for him. He went at once towards Hermies, and, by good luck, came across the tank. It was all closed up. Inside was Thorburn badly wounded, and the crew, most of whom were wounded too, all helpless, not knowing where they were. Under Gerrard's guidance, they got the tank back. The surviving machines of the

M

Composite Company had made their way back from the Quarry through Bus, either on the 22nd or 23rd; but when it became impossible to take them further, they had been destroyed at a "crossroads."

On the 21st, the Padre had superintended the removal of the officers' kit from the Nissen huts, and had formed a dump at Courcelette. On the 22nd, Glanville got orders from the Colonel to go back to Courcelette, to take charge of the dump under the supervision of the Padre. Owing to the advancing enemy, the dump was to be moved further back on the 23rd; but the Padre was sleeping in the lorry and would not be disturbed, so that valuable time was lost, and the kit was not got away. Troops marching along the road made an attempt at looting the dump, and Glanville remained all night on guard. The next day, or rather night, the kit went up in flames along with the tanks!

As we plodded along the Bapaume-Albert road, Gerrard told me, with many excited expressions of regret, of a store-hut full of fur coats, on which he had cast longing eyes, but which regulations forbade him to loot, and compelled him to leave for the enemy. The sky on our left was lit up by Very lights, showing that the enemy was only about a mile away. It seemed that we were not increasing the distance between him and us. After pushing on for three or four miles through darkness, lit only by star shells, a welcome halt was called. The night was bitterly cold. Gerrard and I wrapped ourselves in the blanket I had salvaged, and lay down at the edge of a side road. Through cold

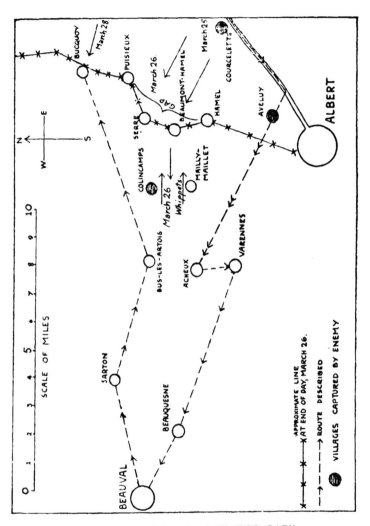

MARCH RETREAT II. "AT THE GAP"

and exhaustion I began to shiver—we had nothing except the clothes we were wearing. Gerrard, who was always ready for a jest, inquired: "What the devil's wrong with you? Have you got the wind up?" How long we rested there I do not know. Eventually, we were told to make for the Tank Corps Driving School at Aveluy, about a mile on this side of Albert.

The wooden huts were deserted. It turned out that the whole personnel of the school—including Hughes—had gone up to hold the line.

I did not care where the enemy was. All I wanted was rest and sleep. We had tramped some twenty miles since dawn, and all the anxiety of a rearguard tank action thrown in. That day—the 24th of March—was my 23rd birthday! By that night the enemy had swept through Le Transloy and Gueudecourt almost to Le Sars and the Butte de Warlencourt. Bapaume and Peronne had fallen. But we still held Albert.

4

It is somewhat difficult to write with any degree of detail of the next few days. I seem to remember that on the 25th we suddenly got orders to leave the Driving School at once, and go six miles further back to Acheux. I have a hazy recollection of bivouacking in a field near a dump of kit (not ours), and of an officer who had recently joined us, his mind now unhinged by the strain of the retreat, walking round and round in circles like a dog chasing its tail. Next morning there was a general reorganization. Every available man was commandeered to form scratch machine-gun sections to go into the firing line. Gerrard and Major Blackburn were amongst those sent up in command. Gerrard went in between Beaumont-Hamel and Serre, where there was a dangerous gap. The previous afternoon the enemy had taken Courcelette, crossed the Bapaume-Albert road, and was pushing westward through this gap in the line which was very sparsely held. Blackburn went in at Colincamps in the area of the gap, but a little further back.

I was sent to Varennes, a mile-and-a-half south of Acheux, to take charge of five tanks. I was to report to Major Bennewith, who had taken over the third company of our Battalion from Major Pratt. These five tanks were all crocks, and, I imagine, came from the Driving School at Aveluy. There was the rumour that enemy tanks were in the neighbourhood, so I half-expected orders to turn and engage them. Few, if any, of the officers, or composite crews, under me, belonged either to my Section or Company. I had to get the tanks back to Beauval, ten miles from Varennes. As we trekked across green fields, I had plenty of time to revolve in my mind the disaster of the last few days. I experienced a sense of loneliness away from the crowd I knew, and regretted that Pratt was no longer in charge of the third company. In my depression, it seemed to me that I was taking part in another Waterloo, where this time the British Army were the vanquished. Across a fifty-mile front it was the Kaiser's battle, and Paris was being bombarded. Although we kept a sharp lookout, there was no sign of enemy tanks, and we stayed the night, as far as I remember, at Beauquesne. I felt badly in need of a pick-me-up, and told Kydd to see if he could get hold of some champagne—though it was not a habit of mine to indulge in such luxury. It seemed a pity to miss the opportunity, since I was for the moment in a peaceful part of France. Kydd duly appeared with a bottle and I felt better after it.

The 26th of March proved to be an important date in the War, for on that day, in the words of Sir Douglas Haig: *"the Governments of France and Great Britain decided to place the supreme control of the operations of the French and British forces in France and Belgium in the hands of General Foch, who accordingly assumed control."*

Even I could see that there was a need for more pulling together, and here was a way to accomplish it. I do not know why, but I had a feeling of complete confidence in this French General. I suppose it was because he had risen purely and solely by his merits as a soldier. I was certain he was the man for the job.

On the afternoon of the 27th we reached Beauval, where I reported to Major Bennewith. After parking the five tanks in a field where there were others, I found a billet in the village. The rumour about the enemy tanks was exploded. They turned out to be our own new light tanks, known as whippets, which had been in action for the first time, in the area of the gap. Owing to their shape being different from that of the heavy tanks, the mistake had arisen.

I learnt now that Albert was lost, and that the

leaning Virgin had fallen.   The German Army was at Amiens.

Was it the end of the War?

## 5

Beauval was a second turning-point for me in the retreat.

Next day, the 28th March, we got orders to leave the tanks there and go forward again.   The enemy was still making determined efforts to open the road to Amiens by capturing the area north of Albert. We were now mobile sections of Lewis gunners, to be rushed where necessary by motor lorry.

We were driven to Sarton, five miles eastward from Beauval.   I have a vivid memory of the lorry entering the village.   It was a peaceful spot, unmarked by war, except for the stir of military. The lorry stopped, between leafy evergreens, on the main thoroughfare.   We got out and turned off along a tree-lined road to the right.   A few yards along was a well-kept farmhouse with a courtyard. The men were billeted in barns, and I found quarters in the farmhouse itself.

I had managed to send three or four field post-cards home since the commencement of the German thrust with the usual, "I am quite well."   Now I seized this, the first opportunity, to write a letter.

*. . . As usual we have been in the thick of it, and except for a slight touch of mustard gas from a shell which fell close by me on the 21st, I am quite well. . . .   From four-thirty a.m. on the 21st, till*

*last night, the 27th, we have been preparing to scrap, scrapping or trekking with practically no sleep and very little rest. I feel absolutely tired out, and we have not finished yet. I am writing this in a French farmhouse, supposedly resting, but we may have to move up again at any moment. Don't wish me many happy returns of the 24th! I don't ever wish to spend another birthday like the last, fighting the whole day a rearguard action whilst the infantry retired. The tanks did wonderful work, and have added fresh laurels to their fame. As usual, I have had most wonderful luck, moving about as though with a charmed life. I don't think this War will last much longer now. The knock-out blow will shortly be dealt. Who will deal it, still remains in the balance. When I think of the German success, I remember our initial success at Cambrai, and also the reverse we suffered shortly after. If we can only deal the Boche now such a blow as he dealt us then, but on a larger scale, we should knock him clean out. Can we? If we don't, God knows what will happen! I fear the worst. I have just received your letters of the 15th, 16th, 17th, 18th and 19th. No, the parcels have not arrived yet, but that is not surprising in view of the present situation! I have seen yesterday's "Daily Mail," which takes a very optimistic view of the situation. More optimistic than I do. Things, in my opinion, are very serious.*

Shortly after our arrival at Sarton, I heard that King George had motored through the village that day during his visit to the Western Front at this critical time.

I have no very distinct recollection of the hour of our departure from Sarton; but leave it we did by motor-lorry for Bus-les-Artois, five miles nearer the line. I believe we arrived there in the early hours of the morning of the 30th. As Lewis gun sections we were ordered into the trenches. My instructions were to report to the infantry brigade in the Bucquoy area between Albert and Arras. There the enemy had attacked and been repulsed on the 28th. It was slightly north of the gap between Hamel and Puisieux which had existed on the 26th, to which Lewis gun sections had been sent from Acheux.

My Lewis gun sections (I think there were about five) and I, were taken part of the way by lorry; but I only remember the end of the journey. In a steady drizzle, we were dumped on a road in the devastated area. Eventually, I found the Brigade H.Q. There I was told that the Lewis guns would help to strengthen the line, and that a battalion of infantry were holding very lightly a wide front. A runner was instructed by the brigade to show me the way to the Battalion H.Q. By this time it was well into the afternoon of a dismal, wet day. Burdened with guns, ammunition and full kit, we straggled along a metalled road. The guide at last turned to the right, and we stepped down into an old disused trench. The bottom of the trench was a morass of gluey mud. We slipped and skidded, and more than once I fell flat in it. We all did. The men struggled to keep the Lewis guns clear of the mud. If the mechanism became clogged, they would be useless. To make matters worse, we had been spotted by the enemy as we had got down into the trench. A battery of light guns got on to us. The air was alive with shells. Whizz-bangs screamed and burst savagely on top of both sides of the trench. The journey had all the horror of a nightmare, in which one seems glued to one spot, and escape from a pursuing terror is impossible. Every step forward was followed by a "clop," as we struggled against the horrible suction which held our feet fast in the mud. Each moment I expected to hear the dreaded cry: "Man hit!"

My next recollection is of having reached the dug-out entrance of the Battalion H.Q., and going down the steps to the bottom. The Colonel welcomed the Lewis guns and ammunition. They needed both. He remarked that we had evidently been observed, for shells had been bumping on the top of the dug-out. He was amazed that we had done the journey in daylight, because a large part of it was in full view of the enemy. I handed over my sections to the infantry. There was no proper trench system, and the line was being held in water-filled shell-holes, which could only be reached over the top. As it was now dark, the sections, each under its officer, were guided to their positions at once. When they were all placed, I went back, according to instructions, to Brigade H.Q., accompanied by my runner. I made my report to the brigadier, and he told me to remain there in case of any orders. On learning my name, he asked if I were any relation of General Hickie*. I replied that our names were spelt differently, and that I thought not. He told me that General Hickie was

*Major-General Sir William Bernard Hickie, K.C.B., commanded 16th (Irish) Division.

interested in anyone of his name, as he belonged to a very old Irish family. The name was prominent at the time, because of the publication of an eighteenth-century manuscript, *Memoirs of William Hickey.*

I was soaked to the skin, and caked in mud. My boots were oozing water. Thankful not to have to make the same journey again that night, I crawled below the bottom bunk in the dug-out. The telephone was in continual use, and I remember a conversation between a staff officer and a Battalion H.Q. in the line. The subject was the disposal of some "dead men." Evidently their burial was overdue, and their condition likely to be insanitary. The utter callousness of the conversation brought home to me that there was precious little respect for a rotting corpse, or glory attaching to it. My last coherent thought was that I should probably be terribly ill through sleeping in wet clothes.

On Easter Sunday, the 31st of March, some time after half-past seven in the evening, I received orders from Major Bennewith to withdraw my Lewis gun sections that night, and with them to march back to Bus-les-Artois. There had been no attack in this sector while we had been there. Under cover of darkness I collected them together and got them back. Very glad we all were to leave the line. I did not envy the infantry, and thanked God I was with the tanks.

According to *The Times* on the 31st of March, the Germans, after ten days' battle, called by the Kaiser the "greatest in history," claimed 75,000 prisoners, and about 1,000 guns.

## 6

The 2nd of April found me once more with the Company, now at Eclimeux, beyond St. Pol, in the Tank Corps Rest Area.

My first consideration was to visit Ordnance, and obtain some fresh underclothing. For the last fourteen days I had not been able to take my clothes off. Much to my surprise, I had not even caught cold, after being obliged to let my wet things dry on me.

Two days later, I wrote home: *Your anxiety for my safety can cease forthwith. I am well out of the danger zone now. . . . I am at present billeted with the Curé of a small French village miles behind the line, sleeping in the greatest comfort between sheets. The memory of the last two weeks is just like a nightmare.*

It so happened that the next day, the 5th of April, the enemy did attack at Bucquoy, and gained the eastern portion of the village, but the advance was stemmed.

I found myself in a Company that seemed strangely altered.

Gerrard was not there. As usual, he had gone one better than I had, and had got a "Blighty" one at Beaumont-Hamel, the day I went up to Bucquoy. Glanville told me that he had been with him at the time. They were in a sunken road having a look round, when a shell exploded near them. Gerrard's sixth sense must have temporarily deserted him, for he exclaimed he was hit, in the back. Glanville had a look but could see no mark, and said disbelievingly, "Nonsense!

There's nothing the matter with you!" Gerrard
persisted that he had been hit; surely he ought to
know. He took off his Sam Browne belt, and sure
enough there was a tiny hole. Glanville did not
think much of it, but Gerrard went back to have
it attended to. A few days later we heard that he
was still in France, unable to be moved. In
addition to being seriously wounded by shrapnel
in the lung, he had been machine-gunned in the
buttock and foot. It would be some time before
he could get to England. It seemed strange now
not to hear his laugh and enjoy his cheerful company. His going left a blankness and loneliness
as far as I was concerned, all the more so since half
the Company now consisted of officers who had
recently joined us.

Glanville told me, too, of a peculiar coincidence.
He reminded me that at Bovington Camp, there
had been an enormous relief map of the Serre and
Beaumont-Hamel area, to illustrate an early action.
It was in that very area, which they had studied
so intensively, that Gerrard's Section had gone in
to hold the line as Lewis gunners.

Another personal loss which I suffered as a
result of the retreat, was Kydd, my batman. The
prolonged marching of the last two weeks had
reopened an old wound in his leg, and he now had
to go into hospital. In his place I got Gerrard's
servant.

My Section had been badly depleted, almost
half of them having become casualties, though
fortunately none had been killed.

Spray now left us. He had received his overdue promotion, and was transferred as a company

commander to another battalion. He had told me that he would try to have me transferred to his new Company to be his second-in-command. Edwards, because of his seniority, became acting Second-in-Command of our Company. I was now the senior, and sole remaining Section Commander in the Battalion out of the original twelve who had left England. The others had either been promoted or become casualties.

Viveash had taken over Gerrard's section, and so received well-earned promotion. A fellow who had been into action five times with the same tank deserved his Captaincy! "Hong Kong," under his command, with the three of my section, "Hadrian," "Havoc," and "Hermosa," had shown more than once what tanks could do when properly used, and they had finally gone down fighting.

.     .     .     .     .

Life was still one continual move!

After five nights at the Curé's, I was sent to the Technical School of Instruction at Bermicourt, on a week's course. Bermicourt was one of the villages of the Tank Corps Principality, in fact it was its capital, for it was the headquarters of General Elles, commanding the Tank Corps. It was only a few minutes by car from Eclimeux.

The object of the course was instruction on the new tank, known as the Mark V, which was superseding the Mark IV. Although similar in appearance to the Mark IV, it was of an improved type. A 150 h.p. Ricardo engine replaced the 100 h.p. sleeve-valve Daimler engine. The new engine was noisier as it had poppet valves. The Mark V had a maximum speed of seven or eight miles an hour, and was more easily manœuvred, the steering being under the sole control of the driver. The two gearsmen of the Mark IV were dispensed with, owing to the epicyclic secondary gears, which were worked directly by the driver. The crew consisted of an officer and five men.

On Thursday, the 11th of April, three weeks exactly from the commencement of the German offensive, and while I was still at Bermicourt, General Sir Julian Byng, commanding the Third Army, sent a letter to General Elles, commending the services rendered by our Brigade of tanks. *"Throughout the operations of the Third Army,"* he wrote, *"from March 21 to April 9 the personnel of the 2nd Tank Brigade have displayed a devotion to duty, a quick appreciation of the battle, and a conspicuous gallantry in helping to save critical situations which I most deeply appreciate. I am proud to have them under my command."* On the same day, Sir Douglas Haig issued *"To/All ranks of the British Forces in France,"* his famous *"With our backs to the wall"* Army Order, which in plain words revealed how serious the situation was: *". . . Victory will belong to the side which holds out the longest. . . . There is no other course open to us but to fight it out! Every position must be held to the last man: there must be no retirement. With our backs to the wall, and believing in the justice of our cause each one of us must fight on to the end. The safety of our Homes and the Freedom of mankind alike depend upon the conduct of each one of us at this critical moment."*

The following night I had supper with a brother
officer at the local estaminet. The meal consisted
of an omelette of eight eggs, a bottle of red wine,
bread, butter, jam and coffee with milk, at a total
cost of 13 francs 50, or in English money 10
shillings and 10 pence. Such an outing made a
pleasant break in the monotony. Two or three
French civilians of the peasant class came along
the street and stopped at the door of the estaminet.
They had evidently been caught in the Retreat, and
were excitedly discussing their experiences, with
many gesticulations. In the confused babel—for
they all seemed to talk at once—the word most often
repeated was "mêlée." I wondered if the Boche
was through near us.

An examination on the morning of Saturday,
the 13th, finished the course of instruction. For the
last three days I had been looking forward to going
to the sea-side camp at Merlimont for a week's
gunnery course there, and I hoped that the new
offensive up north would not interfere with this
plan.

.    .    .    .    .

Contrary to my expectations, in view of the
renewed fighting, I did arrive at Merlimont to
attend the course on the Hotchkiss gun, which
replaced the Lewis gun in the Mark V tank.
Actually, I was now nearer the coast of England
than I was to the front line.

Merlimont, about half-way along the coast
between Le Touquet—Paris-Plage and Berck
Plage (some four miles from each), consisted of
straggling rows of bungalows and villas, scattered

N

over the sand-dunes. Most of the houses were now empty, but were probably the summer homes of families of middle-class "bourgeois." I was billeted in one of them, having a room to myself with a window facing the sea. The house itself was actually on a sand-dune. In the picturesque language of a recent guide-book I could see from my window the "golden sands stretching on either side to a distance of over six miles." I remembered holidays of my childhood spent at Mar del Plata, which to me had been a paradise.

I made the most of my free time while at Merlimont to explore the neighbourhood. Most of one's travelling on these trips was done by "lorry-hopping." When there wasn't a lorry, one walked. I got as far as Étaples, Le Touquet—Paris-Plage, and Berck Plage.

Beside the road to Étaples was—and is—the British War Cemetery, one of the largest in France, At that time, thousands of little white wooden crosses covered acres of ground. Since then, it has been transformed into a lovely spot, beautifully laid out, where about 5,000 British dead are buried. It lies in a hollow between the sea and a ridge of sand-dunes, and is surmounted by an enormous mass of grey stone which stands at the entrance. It is just a large garden, in summer ablaze with flowers, where instead of wooden crosses plain white stones nestle in twos as though to keep each other company. It seems like a resting place where all are asleep, not dead.'

Among my duties at Merlimont, was the censoring of letters. In doing a batch of a hundred I was amazed at the confident spirit of the men with regard to a speedy and victorious finish to the War. I, too, had begun to feel convinced, in spite of moments of utter despondency, and in spite of the blunders we had made in the past (which made my blood boil when I thought of them), that we were going to win. Having seen what had happened on the 24th of March, and how hopeless an Army became once it was disorganized, I believed that a Great Attack by which we could disorganize the enemy, would end in a complete rout for him. Now that we had a Generalissimo, it was my opinion, a great military victory would decide the War.

I was feeling much better for my rest at the sea-side. I had time to study and criticise the War at leisure and at a safe distance in the proper arm-chair manner, by far the most comfortable way of doing so. But what was going to happen to me in two or three days' time I did not know. "Fortune est femme," they said over there, but I hoped she would continue to treat me kindly.

.        .        .        .        .

April the 21st was a Sunday, and I believe I returned to Eclimeux and my comfortable billet at the Curé's then—just a week to the day since I had left it.

I was put in charge of the St. Pol tank defences. I had three tanks under my command, and one was placed on each of the three main roads leading out of St. Pol towards the enemy. The plan was that in the event of a sudden-advance on the town the tank would be driven across the road to block it, and used as a fort from which to blaze into the enemy. The crews lived at farmhouses near-by, and I visited them each day, getting from Eclimeux to St. Pol and from tank to tank by means of a box-body placed at my disposal for the purpose.

There was a fresh Boche offensive on the 24th on the whole British front south of the Somme, in front of Amiens. After drenching the place with gas the enemy attacked with I believe about fifteen tanks and broke through south of Villers-Bretonneux. Spreading north and south his tanks opened up the way for the infantry, so that they captured the village. In this area, near Cachy, the first tank duel took place, when three British tanks engaged three enemy tanks. Two of our machines were females and they were destroyed, but the male tank, commanded by Second-Lieutenant F. Mitchell, although he and the crew were half-blinded by gas, caught the enemy broadside at about 300 yards' range and knocked out one of them with three direct hits and routed the other two. Next day Villers-Bretonneux was in our hands again, being recaptured by the Australians by a daring attack at night.

I had been with the Battalion for a year-and-a-half, in fact, since its beginning, and all that time, except for a week or two at Bovington, I had been a section commander and entitled to the rank of captain, though I did not receive it until after six months' service. I had now been out in France for eight-and-a-half-months and had gone through almost all the actions the battalion had been engaged in. From Junior I had become Senior Section Commander. In spite of this I was still only "Acting Captain whilst commanding a section." The unfairness of this was that if I were wounded, and had to leave the section, I should drop immediately to my substantive rank of "full loot."

We had by now received the Mark V tanks and the Company had been reorganized and refitted. A day or two before the end of the month there were indications of an impending move. It seemed that a big tank battle, tank fighting tank, was anticipated in the Amiens area, and on May the 1st we entrained at Erin for that part of the front.

Both we and the Germans now had tanks, and the tank had become an accepted weapon of warfare.

Sir Douglas Haig acknowledged their proved capability both in defence and attack. In his Dispatch of the March Retreat he said: . . . *Throughout the whole of this fighting tanks took part in numerous successful counter-attacks, many of which were instrumental in checking the enemy's progress at critical points. On these occasions Tanks have shown that they possess capabilities in defence little, if at all, less than those which they have already proved in attack. In their first encounter with German Tanks officers and men of the Tank Corps displayed with success,* under conditions new in warfare, *the same energy and resource which have always characterized their action.*

# CHAPTER VII

ANTI-TANK DEFENCES. WAITING FOR A
TANK *v.* TANK BATTLE AT VILLERS-
BRETONNEUX, IN FRONT OF AMIENS

I

RAILHEAD was at Poulainville, about four
miles north of Amiens. We detrained there
on May the 2nd, and trekked to Querrieu
Wood, about four miles distant. This wood was on
the Albert-Amiens road, some four miles east of
Amiens. It was with a strange feeling that we
bivouacked there with the tanks, for on other
occasions when we had passed it by car the wood
had been a welcome landmark, a sign that we were
approaching Amiens with its civilization and
luxuries. Now Amiens was deserted and was
being continually shelled.

Our line had been formed in front of Villers-
Bretonneux, some seven miles east of Amiens, and
the enemy had been held there. It was of the
utmost importance not to let him capture the
Villers-Bretonneux-Cachy ridge, which formed
part of the outer defences of Amiens. From that
high ground the town was in full view. If the
enemy got there it would be a serious disaster.
Even then the Paris-Amiens-Boulogne railway
could not be used for traffic. "The general situa-

tion . . . was still such as to cause our High Command a certain anxiety." It was on this Cachy ridge the first tank *v.* tank battle had taken place on April the 24th. It was conjectured that that minor effort had been merely an experiment on the part of the enemy with his untried machines, and that another attack, but on a large scale with the whole of his tank corps, would follow. In addition he might use against us any of our tanks which he had captured. A mark of three bars— white, red, white—was painted at the front of each side of the machines we were now using to distinguish them. Otherwise, if he did use captured tanks, it would be impossible at any distance to tell one from the other.

We stayed only a day or so at Querrieu Wood, our Company of tanks finally being parked in Tronville Wood, some three miles from the outskirts of Amiens and four miles behind the front line. The wood was still intact and afforded excellent cover for the tanks. It stretched almost unbroken right up to Villers-Bretonneux, the various parts being known as Tronville Wood, Blangy Wood, L'Abbé Wood, and Aquenne Wood.

We moved up forward by night from Poulainville. The Mark Vs moved quickly compared with our former machines, the Mark IVs, and whereas one could walk more or less comfortably to keep pace with a Mark IV, one had to quicken one's step to keep up with the new machines. Not only that, but changing direction was a very easy matter— the driver had only to pull a lever to make the tail of the tank swing round. We were passing a brick cottage when the tanks were told to change

direction. In the darkness it was difficult to judge
the distance and one tank swung round with such
velocity and force that it knocked down the whole
side of the cottage. To make matters worse, the
cottage was occupied by Australians. They rushed
out, thinking it was a new kind of shell which
had come without the usual warning shriek and
explosion. Their language can be better imagined
than described when they realized that it was one of
our tanks which had knocked in the side of their
home. They left the section commander in no
doubt as to what they thought of the crew's
negligent driving. All he could say in reply was:
"Please get out of the way."

Company H.Q. was in a copse some little
distance from Tronville Wood.

The sections were all practically independent,
each having its own particular spot in the wood. I
shared a bell-tent with my three tank commanders
—who had been changed again—and as the
weather continued fine we were quite comfortable.
I had not seen a paper for some time, but as I had
heard nothing startling I supposed there had been
no further serious disaster. What we were going
to do next I did not know. "Sufficient unto the
day . . ."

We had not been long in Tronville Wood when
it was decided that two tanks of the Battalion were
to be stationed forward, practically in the line at
Villers-Bretonneux. I was honoured, two of my
tanks being selected for the job. It was approximately at the spot where the German tanks had
attacked on April the 24th, and the danger spot
where they were expected to attack again in force.

If and when this happened these two emergency tanks would be at hand ready to go forward immediately against the German tanks to break up their advance. In the meantime the remainder of the Company in Tronville Wood would move up to join in the fray.

The ground in this sector was hard and ideal for manœuvring tanks.

We drove the two machines up by night. Grounds came with us. As we were crossing the open fields on the Cachy ridge, between Cachy and L'Abbé Wood, shells began to fall about fifty yards in front of us on the exact route the tanks were to take. I was uncomfortable about it, for I thought that the enemy must have detected us by the noise of the machines. We halted, and the shelling stopped. We took the risk and moved on again. Fortunately, no more shells fell, and we concluded that the shelling was merely promiscuous. We were not far from the lying-up position we were making for on the road between L'Abbé Wood and Aquenne Wood, and without difficulty got our tanks into position. They were placed at the southern end, so that they could easily be got into the open. They were on a level with Cachy, about half-a-mile to the south, and well concealed by the trees of the wood.

The crews remained at the tanks. As section commander, I lived at the battalion H.Q. of the Australian infantry holding the line. There I was liaison officer between tanks and infantry, ready to receive any orders that might be given me by the infantry commander in the event of a sudden attack.

The Australians at this point were the extreme

right of the British Army in France. The troops on
our right were the famous Moroccan Division, the
finest fighters of the French Army. I was invited
to join the Australian Battalion H.Q. Mess. They
were tremendous tea-drinkers, it being a colonial
custom, they told me, to have tea at all hours of
the day. One night, at dinner, fresh rhubarb was
served as a great treat. It had been gathered in the
ruins of Villers-Bretonneux. It was a real luxury
to get fresh food by way of a change from the
eternal bully-beef. Our enjoyment of this unexpected delicacy was scarcely lessened by its being
faintly flavoured with mustard gas.

I and my two crews were relieved by Viveash
and two of his; we took it in turns with three days
in and three days out, although my tanks remained
up all the time.

About the middle of the first half of May I was
not feeling myself. I did not know what was
wrong, but I became terribly depressed. My
depression was increased by Spray's death. He
had been lying in bed in his tent reading by candle-
light, when a stray shell had burst in the camp,
five miles behind the line, and he had been instantaneously killed by a splinter which broke his neck.
I had not forgotten both broken Life-lines in his
hands, but nevertheless his death came as a great
shock to me. I studied my own hands and was
relieved to find that there was only one break in
my right hand at about my age, and this I believed
to have been my accident at Cambridge. The line
in my left hand was absolutely intact. In War it is
often the least expected that comes about.

During a period in the line about the middle of

May I had a look at the Boche tank "Elfriede" that had become ditched in its efforts to get away after the Cachy attack. It had toppled over into a shell-hole—which was now behind our front line—and for some time its tracks had rattled round. It was a very clumsy affair and looked top-heavy. One of our tanks would easily have gone through the shell-hole in which it had capsized.

The next time I was up in the line I learnt that the French had offered the reward of a Croix de Guerre to every man of a volunteer crew which would get the German tank back. An attempt was then being made by night, and at Battalion H.Q. the Australians and myself followed with the greatest interest the reports that came in. The German tank could not be got away under its own power so a British tank had been brought up to haul it back. During the night the volunteer salvage party had succeeded in getting the tank almost upright when dawn was about to break. They had to remove the props and let the tank fall back into its former position and get both themselves and their own tank back before daylight would reveal what they were doing. The next night a second attempt was made, and profiting by their previous experience, they were able to to get the tank on to its tracks and haul it away. It so happened that a German ration party had used this tank as a landmark when marching up. That night, or early morning, after the tank had been moved, the party walked on and straight into our lines with all the rations, and were made prisoners. The German tank was taken back to Paris to collect money for the French War Loan.

Now the Australians felt certain that the attack was imminent because of the movement and noise behind the German lines. They determined to get a prisoner and cross-examine him for information.

The Battalion H.Q. in the line was in a chalk quarry. It was a spacious shelter consisting of galvanized iron sheeting propped against the wall of the quarry, the sides being either of wood or sheets of iron. There was one door opening into the quarry. I was occupying an upper bunk of rabbit-wire and had been asleep for some time when in the early hours of the morning there was a disturbance which woke me. I sat up leaning on my elbow to see what was happening. The commotion was caused by an Australian sergeant bringing in a youthful German. The Australian officers could not speak German so they called in the M.O. —"the doc."—as they called him to act as interpreter.

"Aussies" in the fire-trench had noticed a German wiring party out, and had made a dash over the top to get a prisoner. The wiring-party had heard them coming, and had fled. All but one had escaped. This man's overcoat had caught in the barbed wire and the Australian sergeant had made for him. While the German was struggling to extricate himself from the wire the sergeant had made sure of him by pinning his coat to the ground with his bayonet. He had then brought him back. The German was obviously frightened and his terror was not lessened by the sight of the sergeant standing beside him with fixed bayonet, tentatively testing the point of it from time to time with his thumb. The prisoner had already been searched and his pockets emptied. The contents when placed on the table consisted only of personal letters and family photos. The doctor and other officers questioned him in a friendly but determined way. The cross-examination revealed that the enemy had no intention of attacking but, on the contrary, was expecting us to do so. According to the prisoner the troops in the line were short of food and their "morale" was shaken. At the end of the examination the prisoner asked that his watch should be given back to him. But no watch had been placed on the table. The sergeant insisted he did not know where it was. When the prisoner continued to plead for the return of his watch, because of its sentimental value, the sergeant impressively assured him how lucky he was to have escaped with his life; if he had wanted he could have killed him. The watch had evidently disappeared for good. Finally, orders were given for the prisoner and escort to go back to Brigade for another interrogation.

One evening a shell exploded in the quarry near the door of the shelter. There was the cry I hated to hear, "Man hit!" He was brought in for a temporary dressing before being sent down to the dressing station.

On May the 20th, the third day of one of my periods in the line, I was again ill, and by evening when I had returned to Tronville Wood I was worse. Consequently, I did not "stand-to" next morning at 3.30 as usual, but remained in bed. I found that my complaint was quite prevalent at the moment, and was a sort of trench fever which lasted a day or two and then went off. I was told one generally had two or three bouts of it before it finally disappeared.

All this while we were on tenterhooks waiting for the Boche to attack. I wrote: *You know what it feels like going to have a dip in a river on a very cold day—unpleasant in its anticipation, not too agreeable in its realization, yet satisfactory to look back upon. That's how I feel about this coming scrap. It will be all right once it's over.* It seemed to me that the attack had to come, and I wished we could know the worst.

From time to time we were shelled in Tronville Wood. On these occasions we took sanctuary together with the glow-worms and other insects with which the place was infested, in a small dug-out we had constructed. Though not proof against a direct hit, it would stop splinters. The hurry with which we bundled into the "Black Hole" was almost laughable.

The last week-end in May, when I went up to the line, I found that the quarry had been heavily shelled, and the shelter had been demolished. Battalion H.Q. was now in a cave-like dug-out in the side of the quarry. It was little more than a passage running to right and left of the entrance, at right angles to it. The Battalion, too, had been relieved. The newcomers were again Australians.

My runner was still Bell, who had been with me at Ypres. He was a man double my age, whose hair had turned white during the Retreat. On this occasion when we were in the line, just before dawn one morning, an enemy barrage was put down. The Australians were certain that an attack would follow immediately, and the tanks had to be warned to start for action at a moment's notice. I was to stay with the Colonel until I got definite orders for the use of the tanks. Bell had to take the message. He had about a mile to go, and his route lay along two sides of a triangle. The shelling was so intense that I really did not think he could get through. But he did. And after all, the attack did not come off. The barrage was only a feint.

I now developed my third bout of illness, variously known as trench fever, Spanish influenza, and PUO, the last being the official Army name for it. I lay on a stretcher in the dampness of the dug-out in the quarry with a temperature of 102.5 degrees F., reading *Oliver Twist* by candle-light. I had the nasty feeling that if a shell hit the entrance we stood a very good chance of being buried alive.

On Friday morning, the 31st, a Boche plane was brought down a couple of hundred yards from Tronville Wood. One wing had been clipped by an anti-aircraft gun. The machine whirled round and round, shrieking through the air, and came to earth with a terrible crash. The pilot and observer fell some twenty yards apart and about fifty yards away from the plane. Both were dead, of course, with every bone in their body broken. A few moments after the plane had crashed, a small dog —a dachshund—came running into our bell-tent. His collar bore the name "Fritz," and also had the name and address of a German officer engraved upon it. How the dog had survived was a mystery, for he must have come down in the plane as he did not belong to the neighbourhood.

On June the 9th I was told to proceed the next day to the Reinforcement Depot to take command of a Company for six weeks.

While I was away, the two tanks were removed from Aquenne Wood, but not before they had had a really bad time. After having been up forward for several weeks they were shelled continuously for thirty-six hours with mustard gas. The crews had to stand-to all this time in readiness to counter-attack. The two tank commanders were Hothersall and McAllister. It was practically impossible to keep a gas mask on for so long. In any case, the gas penetrated their clothing and the box respirators. The probability is, too, that when the crews did take off their masks, the wood was so saturated with gas that it would still be dangerous. By the time the crews were relieved they were completely blinded and had to be led back, unable to see their way. They were invalided to England, and eventually recovered their sight. Hothersall, however, was so badly gassed that his heart was permanently weakened.

# CHAPTER VIII

# THE REST CURE. IN COMMAND OF THE TANK CORPS OFFICERS TRAINING AND REINFORCEMENT COMPANY AT LE TRÉPORT

THE Tank Corps Training and Reinforcement Depôt was at Le Tréport, and I duly arrived there on Monday, June the 10th. It seemed almost too good to be true. The sea air had an immediate tonic effect upon me. Although the camp was said to be at Le Tréport it was actually on the top of the huge chalk cliffs beyond Mers-les-Bains, a little seaside town separated from Le Tréport by the river Bresle, which marked the boundary between the provinces of Picardy and Normandy. Mers-les-Bains was in Picardy, and Le Tréport in Normandy, both places separated only by the Bresle, extended round a bay with high cliffs at both ends. While Le Tréport with its narrow streets and old houses lay huddled beneath the cliffs at the south end, Mers-les-Bains spread out over grassy downland rising to the northern cliffs, and consisted of picturesque villas distinguished by their variety of style. The road from the camp to Le Tréport was inland and passed behind Mers-les-Bains. The journey down was all right, but the slope up was a stiff one! The hospitals were situated on the top of the cliffs at the opposite end of the bay from our camp, really above Le Tréport.

All drafts of officers and men from England came to this camp for a certain amount of training before joining the tank battalions in the line, to which they were detailed to replace casualties. The Depôt was under the command of a colonel of the regular army. He had received the D.S.O. in the Birthday Honours for his very efficient work in connection with the camp. And, in truth, it was a model of systematic organization. Without such organization a camp, which dealt with a company of between one-hundred and two-hundred officers, and several companies of men, their training and daily arrivals and departures would soon get into a pretty good tangle.

I was put in charge of the Officers Company, so that all officers arriving came under me until they went up to the line. I had as my Second-in-Command, a captain, who like myself was there on a six-weeks' term, and who took charge of the training department. In addition, there was a "full loot"—a category "B" officer, and more or less permanent, acting as adjutant, who dealt with all the office work. My work comprised superintending the training and the Mess, and keeping general order—acting as a sort of A.P.M. A.P.M.s were not popular people!

The camp itself was not unlike Bovington, consisting of wooden huts. The officers shared cubicles. There was a tank park where practice with tanks was carried out. There were also gunnery courses and the usual drill. In short, it was another military university.

The job was no sinecure, and I found it very worrying. I was responsible for the conduct and good behaviour of between one and two hundred officers. Firmness was necessary. Immediately I took over I scented that there might be a certain freshness on the part of the more refractory element, who would try to take liberties with the new, young "O.C. Officers Company."

Before my first week was out I had to take disciplinary action.

One night after dinner, there was a commotion in the ante-room. I went in and found tables and chairs being thrown about, and a carpet in the process of being lifted from the floor. I called for order, but no one took the slightest notice. I went over to the nearest offender, who it seemed to me was one of the ringleaders, and ordered him to stop throwing the furniture about. He deliberately ignored me. It was patent that the rowdy element was out to defy me, and were testing me just to see how far they could go. Again I told the fellow to stop. His reply, as far as I remember, was to throw another chair across the room. I finally ordered him out. He refused to go. Determined to stand no more nonsense, I got hold of him, and removed him forcibly. When I put him on his feet again outside the ante-room, he tried to return and threatened to strike me. In view of his still defiant attitude, I called for the Orderly Officer, and put the delinquent under arrest.

Next morning he appeared before the C.O., who took a serious view of the matter, in that he had raised his hand to strike a superior officer. I believe he pleaded that he was drunk, and did not know what he was doing. The C.O. decided, however, that the case would have to be tried by Court Martial. The fellow was therefore to be kept under arrest.

The C.O. spoke to me privately in his office, and by his attitude I realized that I, too, was "on the mat." He censured me for having laid hands on the delinquent myself. I should immediately have called the Orderly Officer to do the job, for if the fellow had struck me—his superior officer—it would have been a terribly serious offence. I believe he said the penalty was death.

Whatever the correct procedure was according to military regulations, my method had achieved its object, and I had no further trouble from the officers under my command. I was respected as one who would stand no nonsense. The job was no Rest Cure! It seemed to me that my having only captain's rank (still "acting"), was a handicap. It was really a major's job, and several of the officers in the Company were majors, waiting to be drafted to units in the line.

In spite of my success in maintaining order, I felt that I had been found wanting in the Colonel's estimation. He demanded the proficiency found in the regimental officers of the Old Regular Army, and I had been guilty of a shocking lapse!

About this time, I received a letter from Sergeant Mitchell, who had been with me in every action. He was the right-gunlayer in "Hadrian" in the attack on Fontaine, when the marksmanship of the tank gunners had silenced the German batteries. The letter was dated the 26th June and ran as follows:

*Dear Capt. Hickey, I must thank you very much for the photo of yourself received a few days ago. I am sending it home to be kept along with others as a remembrance, to recall the pleasant side of the War rather than the adverse side, and my happy associations with you. Things are going on very much the same here. There have been the usual alterations in the Section but Mr. Humphreys' and Mr. McCaffrey's crews remain unchanged. The other bus is commanded by a new officer named Mr. Few with Sgt. Vicary as N.C.O.*

*At the present moment everybody is engaged* . . . (The next two-and-a-quarter lines are illegible, having been stroked out either by the officer who censored the letter or by the writer himself.) *No. 5 Section has now been promoted to a fighting section with Mr. Glanville in charge, but without a 3rd star, we having drawn three new buses the other day. I am sure you will be pleased to hear that Cpl. Dunn has received the Meritorious Service Medal, a very popular award with the Section, also Cpl. Muir has been promoted sergeant. All the old boys miss you very much and are anxiously awaiting your return, tho' of course, Capt. Jones is very popular with them and does all he can to help them, but still there is nobody like their old skipper. They all join me in the best of good wishes.*

*Yours sincerely,*

*A. J. Mitchell.*

I had always felt keenly the responsibility for the lives of the men I commanded, and in all the actions I had been in had never risked a life unnecessarily. I felt, too, that in all fairness, I could not ask any man to do something I was not prepared to do myself, and I, therefore, took equal risks with them. This letter it seemed to me showed that the men had appreciated my consideration for them.

Another award in the Birthday Honours, which I did not hear of until after the War, was the M.C. to Spray. The pity was that he was not alive to receive it himself.

In the early hours of the 4th of July, the Tank Battalion I had left, took part in an action with the Australians, when the village of Hamel (about three miles north-east of Villers-Bretonneux) was captured with but slight loss on our part, and the gain of a large number of prisoners. It had been a repetition of the battle of Cambrai in miniature. An outcome of this successful attack was the enthusiasm which the Australians had for our Tank Brigade under General Courage. Henceforward, they would work only with our Brigade, and with no other!

At the end of the third week my second-in-command was returned to his battalion. He was not replaced, and the absence of a Second-in-Command laid a still greater burden of work on my shoulders. I now had to undertake his duties as well as my own.

To make matters worse, after he had gone the Adjutant departed to England on a fortnight's leave, to recuperate from his attack of 'flu. I was now left to run the Company on my own. I brought one of the reinforcement officers into the Orderly Room to deal with the clerical work, which he did

very ably.   I had thought I was coming to the Base
for a rest!

.        .        .        .        .

It was now some four weeks since the regrettable
incident in the ante-room.   All this time the unfortunate officer had been under arrest, awaiting the
Court Martial.   He had been guarded night and
day by another officer, and had been segregated
from the others—a warning to all not to defy
authority.

In the fullness of time, a Court Martial was con-
vened at Dieppe.   Prisoner, escort, witnesses and
everybody else connected with the affair, went in
a large char-à-banc.   The military had taken possession of a house near the outskirts of the town.
After climbing a steep hill, we got out and mounted
numerous steps up to the front door.   The Court
was held in a top room which had a wooden
balcony.   I was called to give evidence.   The whole
proceedings were soon over, for the prisoner
admitted his guilt, pleading drunkenness.   The sentence of the Court would be promulgated in due
course.   At what stage of the proceedings we had
lunch I do not remember.   But lunch for the whole
party had been arranged at the *Hotel Chariot d'Or*
in the *Grande Rue* of Dieppe.   When we adjourned
there, we found that we were all to sit at the same
table—a long one.   This seemed to me incongruous,
so the prisoner and escort were put at a small side-
table.   We returned to camp, and the prisoner still
remained under arrest with escort.   Eventually,
several days later, the whole of the officers of the
Depôt were assembled in the ante-room, and the

prisoner and escort were marched in at the top end to hear the sentence, which was to be announced before them all. The finding of the Court was— "Guilty: severely reprimanded." Whereupon the erstwhile prisoner once again joined in the normal activities of the Depôt.

My time was now up. So far the Colonel had said nothing to me regarding his report about me to Tank H.Q.; but he had applied to my Battalion C.O. for an extension of three days, so that I might have this time free from duty to recuperate before returning to the Battalion. I decided to spend these three days at Dieppe.

．　　．　　．　　．　　．

While at Dieppe I put up at the *Chariot d'Or* in the main street, where we had lunched when in the town for the Court Martial. It was an ancient hostelry built round a courtyard. The only access to the bedrooms on the first floor was by means of an outside balcony which ran right round the yard. It was impossible to sleep with the door open for anyone could come in; it was equally impossible to keep it shut as it provided the chief means of ventilation for the room. One had to compromise by leaving the door open and closing the shutters, which were provided with slits to allow the passage of air. The building has since been demolished and has been replaced by a shop.

The town was absolutely dead. The War had put a temporary stop to holiday visitors. One of the largest hotels was a hospital.

On Monday, the 29th July, my week-end respite ended, and I started off to rejoin the Battalion. I jumped a lorry ride as far as Abbeville, where I got a train to railhead.

There I had to spend the night waiting for transport. Luckily the weather was fine. I put up at an uncouth sort of stable-house in the village. Everything (bed, sheets, pillows) was nevertheless scrupulously clean. The old lady and her daughter who lived there were most hospitable.

Breakfast next morning consisted of three *œufs sur le plat*, bread and butter, coffee, milk and sugar. My hostess would not hear of my paying for it. She insisted that it was all she could do, in her small way, to repay and thank officers going up to the line. If they did not go up, the Boches would be in her house, and what would be the use of money to her then.

I was going to put a five franc note (about four shillings) on the table and say nothing, but she foresaw my intention and begged me not to do so.

This in almost the fifth year of War.

# CHAPTER IX

AMIENS. THE SECTION HEADS THE
AUSTRALIANS IN THE FIRST NIGHT
ATTACK WITH TANKS

I

THAT afternoon I arrived back with the Section at Tronville Wood. After the Retreat Colonel Willoughby had gone back to England on account of ill-health. The new C.O., Colonel Bingham, who had got the D.S.O. for the success of the Battalion at Hamel, inquired how I was feeling, and I replied all right.

It was a pleasant evening walk across the fields from Tronville Wood to Boves on the far side of the Paris-Amiens railway line. The line had a deserted appearance. No trains were running between Amiens and Paris. It seemed strange to think that only three years previously I had travelled in comfort along it on my way to Spain. Now it was merely a broken link with civilization. The village of Boves was deserted, the occupants having fled, leaving most of their personal possessions behind. Not much damage had been done by shell-fire, but there was evidence that there had been looting.

Two or three days after my return all our tanks left Tronville Wood and moved some three miles northwards, through Blangy Tronville to the valley of the Somme. Our position there was always known by its map reference of "o.13.ac." We bivouacked on firm ground in among the trees which grew thickly in the valley, and effectually screened the tanks from observation. We were sheltered on the side nearest the enemy by a high bank—the edge of the valley—and on the other side of us, marshy land interspersed with pools of stagnant water stretched down to the river. Another Company of the Battalion had been there since May, and had installed themselves comfortably in dug-outs made in the bank. The area had been shelled occasionally, but usually the shells had fallen in the canal, doing little or no damage.

On Sunday, the 4th of August, there was a drum-head service for the Battalion. I recollect the Padre's address. It was the fourth anniversary of the declaration of war. During those four years, we had been through much, and it was not to be wondered at that some of us were war-weary. Now, however, we had got reinforcements from England, and their man-power combined with our experience should carry us to victory. An added spur to our flagging spirits was the arrival of the American troops. They had recently been in action for the first time, and "given convincing proof of their high fighting quality." It was in fact a tremendous relief, and almost a moral tonic to feel that here was a nation untired by war ready to pour its manhood into battle.

It was obvious that we were going into a big show. But as everything was being kept secret, I did not know the extent of the battle front. I knew that we would be with the Australians, in a great drive forward on the Amiens front. By the 6th of August we had definite orders for our particular job. I had to prepare for Grounds, the Company Commander, a list of the officers, N.C.O.s and men of my Section who would be retained to go into action. The fact was there had been so many changes that my Section was now only a shadow of its former self; at least that is how it appeared to me. The three Tank Commanders were all reinforcement officers. One of them had been with me at Tronville Wood before I had gone to Le Tréport, but the other two I had not met until I returned. To cap it all, Sergeant Mitchell was transferred out of my Section to become an N.C.O. tank commander in another section; but I was left with two corporals who had risen to that rank under me, one being Corporal Dunn, M.S.M. Few of the men I had had were left. I, therefore, had a Section which, with the exception of two or three members, I had not trained in any way and of whose capabilities I had no idea. I wished I knew them better! Bell, my runner, had been badly shaken both by the Retreat of the 21st of March and onwards (the 24th of March had practically done him in), and by Villers-Bretonneux. He was a man of middle age and appeared to be breaking up. I decided it was time he was relieved and someone else had a turn. From the men available, I selected Stittle, whom I knew to be experienced, efficient and reliable. He had been with the Section throughout, having been a member of "Havoc's" crew. The total strength of the Section going into action was four officers (including myself), one sergeant, two corporals and fourteen men—in all twenty-one. On Section Headquarters there was myself and my runner. Each of the three tanks (they were all Mark Vs) had a crew of an officer and five men. The odd man, making the total strength of twenty-one, was a reserve.

Active preparations similar to those at "Horseshoe Wood" before Cambrai, were carried out at "o.13.ac." On this occasion, however, I did not go over the Approach March route, firstly, because there was no time—I had only just come back to the Battalion, and secondly, the route was to be that taken for the battle of Hamel, a month earlier; in any case, according to the Operation Orders, the Reconnaissance Officer was to be responsible for guiding the tanks to the Company Point of Assembly behind Hamel.

During the preparations, I heard MacFarlane, who was now a captain, letting fly at one of the men of his Section. Evidently the fellow was feeling windy, and was trying to evade going into action by saying he was ill. MacFarlane was openly incredulous, knowing the man was "swinging the lead." His reply to the would-be malingerer was forcible. Lifting a large tool, he said, holding it above the man : "I'll knock you on the head with this spanner if you do not go into action with your tank."

In a magazine I picked up, I came across a symposium of views on our *Life After Death*, or some such heading. It was in the nature of a competition, and each contribution published had secured, I think, a guinea. The poet, A. G. Prys Jones, a friend of mine, now a H.M. Inspector of

Schools in Wales, was among the successful contributors. His view seemed to be that the hereafter was a continuation of our present life but in spirit form. Throughout the War I was rather a materialist. My accident at Cambridge had produced a long period of unconsciousness. It was only the skill of the Medical Officer, Colonel Ballance (later a knight), which saved my life. It seemed to me that death was a form of oblivion from which there was no awakening. When the flame of life was extinguished, all that remained were the ashes, and one's record of achievement.

A strange feature of the War was the premonition some fellows had of approaching death. Bown had had this sense of impending disaster just before going into action on the St. Quentin Ridge, when he asked Gerrard to go in his tank. Now another fellow had the same feeling, and made all his final arrangements. In fact, this attack proved to be the end for him.

As soon as it became dark on the 7th of August we started our Approach March. From "o.13.ac" over the four miles to the Company Point of Assembly behind Hamel, the tanks went, one after the other. As we reached the forward area, a squadron of aeroplanes flew between the lines. This manœuvre was to drown the noise of the tanks moving up. Tea had been brought in containers. Heaven knows how long it had "stood," but for strength I have never tasted anything to equal it. It was now handed round with a stiff lacing of rum. We waited in darkness and silence. Suddenly at four-twenty a.m. (zero hour) our massed artillery opened intense fire on the whole front of attack.

This hurricane bombardment was muffled by the dense ground mist which had risen from the Somme valley and spread like a blanket over the country. It was literally impossible to see one's hand before one.

The attack was divided into two "phases." We were in the second, and were to follow in the wake of the tanks and infantry of the first phase, their objectives—known as the "Green Line"—were to be our jumping-off places. The second phase was not to commence until four hours after zero—eight-twenty.

In the impenetrable mist we started off for our forming-up position beyond Hamel, where we were to fall in with the Australians. I was responsible for getting my Section there. It was impossible to see where we were going, and it was more by good luck than good guidance that when the mist lifted we found ourselves in Hamel. I remember a frenzy of movement on the road there, light guns were being rushed forward. Eventually we reached a field where tanks were lined up. It was with great relief that I found that I was in my correct spot, for I had had visions of a Court Martial because my tanks had failed to get into action through my losing the way. Anyhow that bogy was now completely dispelled, for I saw in front of me Colonel Bingham and the R.S.M. on horseback, the latter bearing the Battalion colours. Each tank also carried the Battalion flag. It was, in fact, the forming-up position.

The first phase, it appeared, had been a great success. The enemy had been taken completely by surprise, and tanks and infantry had simply smashed through. Now, at a given signal, we started off in brilliant sunshine across the newly acquired ground towards the "Green Line," about two miles ahead.

2

We arrived there on the ridge south of Cerisy with time to spare. To the north was a sharp downward turn of the twisting Somme, and to the south the great east-west road from Amiens to St. Quentin seemed to run straight as far as the eye could see. As at Cambrai, we were in the centre of the battle front. The Australians had on their left English troops, and on their right the Canadian Corps, with the French First Army still further along.

While we waited, I noticed a group of Australians beside a still form lying on the ground. As I watched, they dug a shallow trench and buried their dead comrade, just as he was in battle array.

With this picture in my mind, we started into action. The pace of the advance was regulated by the progressive lifting of the artillery bombardment from specified places. While other sections had been allotted to particular battalions, mine was more or less a free agent. Its duty was to assist in reducing all strong-points on a frontage of about three-quarters of a mile immediately south of the Somme and occupied by two Australian Battalions, each of which already had a section of tanks allotted to it. As we started at eight-twenty a.m. the barrage lifted from the valley in front of us. Enemy machine-guns were chattering in the woods on the right. I thought we were in for a sticky time. I could see Glanville going forward with his tanks ahead of the infantry. Wearing a Burberry, his tin hat jammed down over his eyes, and map in hand, he was pointing out the way. It seemed to me that the machine-guns would soon be on to his tanks and he would be wiped out.

My three tanks separated. "H24" (2nd-Lieut. S. S. Jeffries) went off to the left; "H32" (2nd-Lieut. C. E. Few) to the right; while I went with "H25" (2nd-Lieut. H. W. Humphreys) along a middle course. The infantry, keeping well up with the tanks, were advancing in extended order. About half-way to our objective, while passing on the right of Morcourt, I heard the "whizz-whizz, zip-zip" of a sniper's bullets. They struck the earth round about me. When I realized that they were meant for me, I took cover in a shell-hole. Then I went on. We were now on the crest of a ridge, and I could see across the valley to the next ridge which was our objective. The tanks and infantry were moving forward without a hitch. As I passed the entrance to an abandoned German dug-out, I had the momentary thought of going inside to get a souvenir. Then I decided no. All this time one could hear the chatter of machine-guns. What surprised me was that the line steadily advanced and that no one fell dead.

It was now about 9.20 a.m. This part of the Somme valley was lovely country. Ridges and valleys succeeding one another, stood out in relief in the clear morning air. "Proud and rich in the sun's eyes," the dark green of woods showed up against the paler shades of fields "gay with gold."

P

The silver thread of the Somme wound through the countryside, between Cerisy and Chipilly, and past Morcourt, all set on its banks. From Morcourt a winding white road led over the ridge to Proyart —beyond our objective.

By 10.20 a.m. our infantry were on the "Red Line"—our objective—the ridge beyond Morcourt, about two miles east from our jumping-off place on the "Green Line." The work of our tanks was, therefore, finished, for the infantry were digging themselves in along the top of the ridge. The Somme on our left at this point made a deep bend in our direction. On the spur of land across the river an enemy field-gun—east of Chipilly—suddenly burst into action. Each time the gun fired I could see the spurt of flame, hear the scream of the shell, and then the explosion. "H25" was sheltered by a slight curve in the ridge, but one of Glanville's tanks was in full view of the gun which was firing at it. The shells were exploding perilously close, and I could see that the tank would be hit pretty soon if it were not withdrawn at once from its exposed position. As far as I could make out the crew of the tank did not know they were being fired at. Rapidly I calculated that by the time the tank crew had the enemy field-gun indicated to them, sighted their guns, taken aim, and fired, perhaps having to correct their range before they secured a hit, the tank would be knocked out. I hurried to Glanville and pointed out the danger to him, of which I think he was unaware. He replied that there was a machine-gun ahead which was doing mischief. I do not know if he knew exactly where it was, but he was determined to wipe it out. I

urged that it was more important for him to get
his tank to cover; his infantry were on the "Red
Line," and the next wave of tanks would deal with
the machine-gun ahead. As a matter of fact, the
big Mark V "Star" tanks were leap-frogging
through us towards their objective, the "Blue
Line," which they were to exploit about a mile
further on. Glanville still hesitated, hankering after
the machine-gun. The enemy field-gun was now
bracketing frantically on his tanks which was a
splendid target. Closer and closer fell the shells.
I urged Glanville to hurry up. All this took place
in the space of seconds. Suddenly, as I was leaving
him, a shell passed over his tank and exploded
close to me. Automatically I ducked, and this
instinctive action saved my life. A fragment of
shell struck my back. Gingerly I explored the spot
with my fingers. My tunic was torn! My thoughts
flew back to Gerrard's wound. It had seemed
nothing at the time and yet it had proved serious.
I could feel a lump rising, and wondered if I had
got a splinter. Glanville now got his tank under
cover and the gun stopped firing.

My job being done I went back to see the
Medical Officer whom I met walking up towards
the tanks. He examined my wound and dressed it,
telling me that although it looked nasty it was not
serious. The piece of high explosive which had
struck me had just ripped my tunic and caused a
flesh wound, but no particle of metal had entered.

My three tanks rallied with the other survivors
in the shelter of a steep grassy bank on the side of
this ridge east of Morcourt, very close to the "Red
Line." "H32" had reached its objective without

incident, except for the unpleasantness of bad ventilation and fumes which had affected the crew; but
"H24" had met with opposition in the neighbourhood of Morcourt, and Corporal Dunn had been
severely wounded. Talking over the events of the
morning I heard one or two tales. Glanville,
wanting to get inside one of his tanks had gone
behind it while it was in motion, and put his hand
through the revolver loop-hole to open the rear
door. One of the crew seeing the hand had thought
it belonged to a German. He had seized it and
would not let go. Glanville had been dragged along
at a speed of about six miles an hour. At last he
had made the fellow inside realize who he was and
had been released. In the case of another tank a
German came to the front flaps. He wished to
surrender. The officer signed him to go back. The
German misunderstood and thought he was to get
on the carrier at the rear, which he did. Later, one
of the crew looking out through the rear revolver
loop-hole and seeing a German on the carrier, shot
him dead. This tank shortly afterwards was
knocked out by five direct hits and set on fire.

I heard that Sergeant Mitchell with his tank
"H21" had done excellent work in Morcourt,
enabling his infantry to reach their objective
without a casualty.

The afternoon passed peacefully enough in the
shelter of the bank, and that night we bivouacked
there.

### 3

Next morning one Company of the Battalion
was detailed to go into action again—this time

against Vauvillers, further south. The tanks started off with the Australians about eleven o'clock. As was to be expected, the enemy was not unprepared, and the tanks got a warm reception, several soon being put out of action. The infantry, however, were following up well, and captured the village and established themselves in front of it.

During that day I did not stray far from our encampment, but seized the opportunity to obtain as much rest as possible. Knowing by this time that in an offensive where tanks were used they were never withdrawn until they were fought to a standstill, I anticipated further action in the near future. I could not see that it was serving any useful purpose to allow oneself to be hit through lack of proper caution in wandering over the countryside. Though quite prepared to face danger and death in the performance of a task that was given me, I considered that it was also a duty to avoid unnecessary risk.

That afternoon, Jones and Viveash, who were close friends, strolled up the ridge and sat down to chat. I was resting in the bivouac under the nose of one of my tanks when I heard a voice saying in agonized tones: "Viveash is dead! Viveash is dead!" Looking up I saw Jones at the top of the bank; grief was in his face and he held out his arms in an appealing gesture as he bent forward. My immediate reaction to his cry was: "But Viveash can't be dead. He was here just a short time ago. It can't happen like that!" And then came the realization that Viveash *was* dead. Another of the original twenty-seven gone! Now there were only nine left. Strangely enough when death had come to him it was not in action. His friends buried him, and erected a cross over his grave. We mourned the loss of a gallant officer, through whom the tanks had won glory.

In the evening, following orders received, we moved the tanks about two-and-a-half-miles to Bayonvillers on the south side of the Amiens-St. Quentin road and about four miles from the front line. The village was in ruins, and the tanks were hidden as well as possible by means of camouflage nets, against a hedge.

We spent the night there by the side of the machines.

## 4

So began, on an eleven-mile front, the Hundred Days Battle, which culminated in the Armistice of the 11th November 1918. The whole operation east of Amiens was very much on the lines of the First Battle of Cambrai; but, with defences to attack unimportant compared with those of the Hindenburg Line. The great success of the 430 tanks in action on August the 8th (which Ludendorff himself called the "black day of the German Army") was intoxicating: tanks had penetrated in one place on that day to a depth of seven miles. Tanks now almost seemed to be regarded by responsible Staff Officers as super-terrific monsters which had such a devastating effect on the enemy morale that they could not meet with failure. The lesson had not yet been learned that after an initial attack, the element of surprise, essential to a tank action, had been lost.

On August the 10th, which was a Saturday,

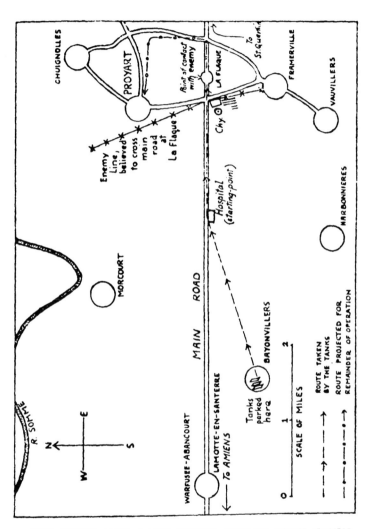

THE FIRST (AND LAST) NIGHT ATTACK WITH TANKS

Jones and I got orders from Grounds to go with
him to the Australian Divisional H.Q., about a mile
away on the north side of the Amiens-St. Quentin
Road. There we met several Staff Officers, and
about half-past three received from them verbal
orders for an attack in which tanks were to
co-operate that night with the 10th Australian
Infantry Brigade. The operation had been so
hurriedly arranged that no written orders were
available. However, my Section was to do the job.
We were to head the 37th Battalion of Australian
Infantry under cover of darkness, against Proyart,
with the object of adjusting an inter-corps
boundary. A second battalion of Australian
Infantry, accompanied by Jones's section of tanks,
was to move up in reserve. Zero hour was fixed
for half-past nine that night, the "starting-point,"
where the tanks were to pick up the infantry, being
a place marked on the map "Hospital," on the
Amiens-St. Quentin Road. This meant that the
tanks had to do the "Approach March" in broad
daylight, a breach of the first principles of tank
warfare!

Proyart was only about half-a-mile beyond the
"Blue Line," and in the neighbourhood of Bray-sur-
Somme, our old winter quarters! The two villages
lay about four miles apart with the Somme flowing
between, Bray, of course, being on the north side.

Instead of making a frontal attack on Proyart,
the plan was to penetrate the enemy line about one
mile further south, where it crossed at right-angles
the Amiens-St. Quentin Road. This was believed to
be at the cross-roads known as La Flaque. After
proceeding along the highway for three-quarters of

a mile, the column was to turn north at a prescribed cross-roads and by an encircling movement attack Proyart from the rear. The tanks were to advance in spear-head formation, one on the road and one about fifty yards away on each side of it, the infantry following along the road. As soon as the whole column had turned north, fast armoured-cars with headlights full-on, were to dash along the Amiens-St. Quentin Road. The idea was to delude the enemy into thinking the attack was in that direction and so put him off the tanks and infantry which had turned northwards.

We who were to take part in this novel operation realized its risks, for tanks had never before been used in an organized night attack. Besides, a great deal had had to be left to chance, for, owing to shortage of time, none of the normal work in the way of preparation and precaution, had been done. None of us had the least idea what the ground was like; and to the disadvantage of the restricted vision from inside a tank, was now to be added the possibility of complete darkness inside and out.

Part of the scheme was that the tanks should go into action with headlights full-on. I remarked that if this were done the exact position of the tanks would be revealed and they would be knocked out before they could do anything, while the enemy still remained unseen in the darkness. This point was eventually conceded.

With a tank on either side of the road, there was the risk that in an engagement the tank gunners would be unable in the dark to distinguish our troops from the enemy, and would fire into the men marching on the road. I remembered what had

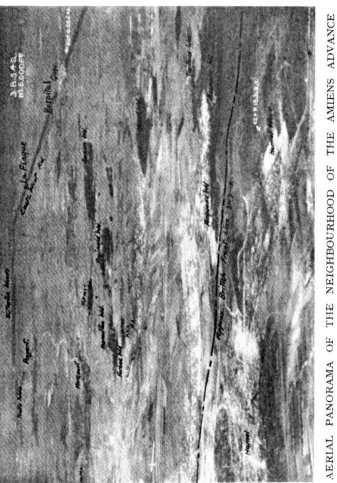

AERIAL PANORAMA OF THE NEIGHBOURHOOD OF THE AMIENS ADVANCE
showing Amiens—St. Quentin Road, Somme, Hamel, Morcourt, Hospital,
La Flaque, and Proyart

happened at Doignies on March the 21st, when the tanks had lost their way in the mist and darkness and were on the point of firing into our own infantry. I realized that in this night attack, if the tanks were not kept on the road, disaster would follow. For, losing direction, they would do the same thing again, only this time perhaps they would actually fire into their own supporting troops. The tanks and infantry would have to keep in very close touch to avoid this danger.

There was, in addition, every possibility that the tanks moving in the dark over unknown ground at the sides of the road would be ditched. As far as I could see, the only way to get over this difficulty was to adopt the method used in night "approach marches." On such accasions a man had walked in front picking out the way and guiding the tank by the glow of a cigarette. But this suggestion was greeted with the remark who would supply the cigarettes?

Also, it was certain that the enemy would now be prepared to meet tanks with artillery, anti-tank rifles and armour-piercing bullets, especially at a place where his line crossed the main-road.

It seemed to me that the whole operation had very little chance of success, because it was at every stage against common sense and was fraught with great danger. Risks can only be justified when it is certain that everything possible in the way of preparation and precaution has been done.

As I have said, my tanks were carefully camouflaged in a hedge in the derelict village of Bayonvillers, a distance of about two-and-a-half miles from the Hospital. On the way up, as we trekked across the fields, we saw an enemy plane up aloft on our left above the road. We took cover by some trees, and wondered if the tanks had been spotted, as it was broad daylight. At eight o'clock, having reached the rendezvous, I reported to the commanding officer of the 37th Battalion, as previously arranged, and was told that Zero hour had been altered to ten o'clock, therefore I was not to bring my tanks into position at the head of the infantry until a quarter-past nine.

The following is Major Heseltine's account of how the 37th Battalion received its orders for this night action:

-*During the attack on August 8, 1918, the 37th Bn. was in reserve, and consequently took no active part in that battle, but was moved up in rear of the fight, and on the evening of that eventful day bivouacked in a steep gully at Morcourt, near the Somme, where it remained till August 10.*

*On the morning of the 10th the Commanding Officer (Lieut.-Colonel Knox-Knight) was sent for by brigade headquarters, and returned about 2 p.m. I was his adjutant, and when he came back he told me to make arrangements for the Battalion to move that evening. Each man was to carry two days' rations in addition to his usual 'iron rations,' as well as extra ammunition, grenades, 'Very' lights, rockets, etc. While I was arranging this he saw the Battalion Scout Officer and the Company Commanders and explained the task the Battalion had to carry out.*

*It was, I think, about 5 p.m. when the Battalion*

*Reveille,* February 1934, "Tanks in Night Stunt," by Major S. H. Heseltine.

*moved off, and while we were marching the Commanding Officer explained the scheme to me as he had not had an opportunity of doing so before.*

*He said that the 10th Infantry Brigade, with some tanks attached, was to march out that night along the Amiens-St. Quentin Road, the 37th Bn. leading, and at a certain point behind the German front line we were to wheel to the left. That at the same time another force on our left was to move in a similar way, but to wheel to its right, so that the two forces would meet head-on, and when they did so everybody was to halt and dig in on the ground they were on and to face both ways. The idea of the operation was to surround an area of ground held by the Germans. Other troops were then to advance from our original front line and drive the Germans who were in the area enclosed by us into our arms.*

Be this as it may, I did now know it at the time.

At the appointed hour, the tanks, "H24," "H25," "H32," in that order, moved forward in the twilight at the head of the infantry, who followed in single file. We had about one-and-a-half miles to go before we reached La Flaque. On seeing the actual ground which the tanks would have to negotiate on either side of the road, it was obvious that they simply could not do it. All along both sides of the road were old trenches, earthworks and dumps. At one place there were huts and at another a railway siding. It would have been difficult enough, if not impossible, for tanks to traverse this ground in daylight. By night, it was out of the question. In addition, the road was lined with trees, which would make it practically impossible for the tanks at the sides to keep in touch with the infantry. On my map was a footnote which warned me that: "The fact that an obstacle is not represented on the map does not necessarily mean that there is none there. It is often impossible to distinguish obstacles or to identify their character. It may be assumed that there are obstacles in front of all fire trenches (shown by thick line)." Tanks were very vulnerable where certain obstacles were concerned. A buckled underplate caused by a tree-stump could easily foul the fly-wheel of the engine (I believe there was only a quarter of an inch clearance) and put the tank completely out of action. After consultation with the Australian Colonel, it was agreed that all three tanks should keep to the road. In spite of our orders, there was nothing else for it. The infantry Reconnaissance Officer was appointed by the Colonel to be responsible for direction, especially for the exact point where the whole column was to turn north after piercing the enemy line. The Colonel instructed me to accompany him so that I should be at hand if he wished to give any particular orders for the tanks.

As I walked with him ten to twenty yards behind the tanks, he said to me: "There will be a train-load of V.C.s waiting for us when we get back, if it's a success. But," he added, "we won't want them—if we get through with our lives." Fifteen years later, Humphreys told me that while we were waiting at the "Hospital" to start off, the Colonel talking to several officers sitting on the bank at the side of the road had told them the same thing. We adjusted our pace so as to reach La Flaque about ten o'clock, when it would be sufficiently dark to proceed.

When we got to La Flaque darkness had fallen. We were all keyed up, expecting opposition at this point. But, to our surprise, we met with none. The Colonel and I wondered if the enemy had withdrawn his line to a point further back, or if the tanks had been observed moving up in the daylight, and he was laying a trap for us. The night sky in front looked peaceful and calm. If the enemy were holding a line at this point it seemed impossible that he should be unaware of our presence, for the clatter of the tanks on the hard road rent the stillness of the night. About a quarter of a mile beyond La Flaque we heard above the noise of the tanks the roar of a plane overhead. Suddenly, there was a downward whizz, a blinding flash and then a terrific explosion. The unditching-beam of the rear tank (as I thought)—about ten yards away—flew up into the air and crashed back. It is difficult to remember exactly the position of the Colonel and myself at the moment this bomb fell. We were certainly on a level with the tanks. It may have been that we were between the second and third tanks, but slightly to one side. When discussing this narrative with Humphreys, whom I had not seen since the attack fifteen years before, he told me that he was certain it was his tank (the second one in the order of advance) on which the bomb had fallen. They had felt the shock inside the tank, and his driver had remarked that that was a bomb. But, until Humphreys saw this narrative, he did not know what had, in reality, happened outside. His comment to me was: "Lucky it fell on the unditching beam!" The bomb had exploded on impact, and the unditching beam, resting loosely on top of the tank had taken the force of the explosion. If the bomb had exploded directly on the tank it would have been the end of it and the crew!

As luck would have it, this was exactly the spot where the enemy was holding his line and had a strong-point in a large dump at the side of the road. Other bombs fell. The noise of the bombing-plane had up to this moment drowned the clatter of the tanks, but now the enemy was alarmed. He at once put up flares which made the night as bright as day. In the ghastly light we could see the poplars and the hedges along the road. Then hell was let loose! A withering machine-gun fire was opened on the tanks. The infantry following close behind, being swept by it, took cover in the ditch on the south side of the road. The tanks replied with their 6-pounder and machine-guns, but without effect, for no targets could be seen. The peculiar thing was that there was not even a flash to aim at. I did not know then that anti-flash devices were fitted to machine-guns. In short rushes the infantry continued to advance. The enemy had now got his artillery to bear on us, and shells began to explode in the road and on either side of it. The noise was terrific. Machine-gun bullets cracked all round like a thousand whips. A War Correspondent, who was in a position to have a full view, described how one of the tanks was lit up like a blacksmith's fire by the quantity of bullets striking it. Hardy and Merrell, as tank engineers, were following us up along the road. They were somewhere between the Hospital and La Flaque when the enemy plane passed overhead and dropped bombs on the road. A motor-cyclist was wounded, and Hardy and Merrell took shelter in a dug-out. A few moments later from where they were they saw the blaze of our night attack. It looked like a Brock's fireworks display. They thought it was all up with us. I had, as a small boy of five or six in the Argentine one night when going along a road, been terrified by fireworks coming through a hedge which we had to pass—much to my father's disgust, although he had picked me up and carried me. Now, instead of fireworks, it was live bullets!

After about half-an-hour there was a short lull, except for desultory firing. The tanks had halted. The Colonel was on the road taking stock of the situation, and I was hurriedly approaching the rear tank to find out what was happening, when Humphreys hastened to me with a terrible wound in his right fore-arm. He was weak from loss of blood and had been obliged to hand his tank over to the corporal. It was obvious he could not carry on, and I sent him back to have his wound dressed. He reported that the enemy were using anti-tank rifles and armour-piercing bullets. Twice the flap of the porthole in front of him had been knocked out of his hand by bullets as he held it open to see outside. The second time he had got the gash in his arm. It was just before he was wounded that his driver was hit in the chest and had been rushed to the back of the tank while it was still in motion. Then the tank hit a tree and the engine stalled. There were frantic efforts to get it going again

Q

and the lights by Humphreys' shoulder were accidentally turned on, drawing more fire. I remember seeing the lights go on, and not knowing what was happening inside, thought: "What bloody fools!"

Humphreys told me it was impossible to locate the enemy machine-guns from inside the tank, and on two occasions when he had got outside to keep in touch with the infantry, he could see nothing. It was not until our talk fifteen years afterwards that he told me that when he climbed out on to the road bullets were flying so thickly that he dived into the ditch for cover, landing on a German! In the light of the flares he could see his grey uniform. He pulled out his revolver to plug him but it was not necessary. The German was a corpse and already cold.

I immediately returned to the Colonel to tell him that I had lost an officer and give him the information I had received.

The tanks started to move again. Immediately there was a hurricane of machine-gun fire, and again we took cover. The night was pitch-black, except for occasional flares. The infantry advancing in short rushes along the side of the road were being mown down like grass, and lay where they fell. At this moment a runner reported that the tanks were returning. "They haven't got orders to turn, have they?" the Colonel asked me in amazement. I was equally staggered, and replied: "Certainly not! I'll go at once and tell them to keep straight on." "Yes, you must," he answered, and standing erect, urged the infantry on. As I made a dive forward, with my runner in a hailstorm of bullets, I heard a choking gasp and saw the Colonel fall heavily to the ground, two feet away from me. While we ran the few yards to the tanks my runner's pack stopped a bullet. Miraculously, he was not injured. He found the bullet later in his pack.

Again, it was not until the fifteen years later that I learned from Humphreys that the tanks had already turned when he met me. The reason for their turning, he told me, was to keep in touch with the infantry, who were nowhere to be seen.

Getting the tanks to go forward again was no easy job. I began with the rear tank, and had to batter on the front with my stick to attract the attention of the officer inside. It was like trying to turn a car in a narrow road, and there was a good deal of manoeuvring and reversing and shouting before the second and third tanks were finally turned. Finding I had my work cut out with them, I sent Stittle (my runner) forward to direct the front tank on again. It appears that Major Heseltine, the Adjutant of the 37th Battalion, was up here at this time, having been sent by the Colonel to get the troops moving forward again. He describes the tanks as looking then each like "a huge firework" owing to the number of machine-gun bullets striking it. Then all at once I found I was about to be jammed between the two tanks as they struggled to get turned round. Frantically I scrambled up the back of one of them, wondering: "How is it I am still alive? Is it worth the struggle? I really ought to be dead by this time!"

I discovered that Jefferies, in charge of the first

tank "H24," was missing since the first few minutes of the engagement. He was last seen by Humphreys on the back of his bus with Lieut. McNicoll, the Australian Scout, or Reconnaissance Officer. I can only think that a shell or a bomb completely obliterated him. I have never heard of his body having been found.

The tank was perforated on all sides by armour-piercing bullets and all the crew, except two, were wounded. It was now in charge of the second-driver, a gunner, Neal, who had manœuvred it for position to engage enemy machine-guns firing from what appeared to be a strong-point. This tank never actually turned round, but it was this manœuvre which the infantry mistook and led them to report that the tank was returning. When Stittle reached the leading tank the men were anxiously awaiting instructions, and asked him what was happening. They were, in fact, waiting, expecting to go forward.

Humphreys' tank, minus its officer and with its driver wounded, had only half its crew uninjured, and was in charge of a corporal. The officer and crew of "H32" were all badly shaken and wounded by splinters, one man, in addition, being gassed by fumes from the exhaust. The reason that the second and third tanks were coming back was that according to specific instructions they must keep in close touch with the infantry, and they had turned to find them. It was no good the tanks going on if the infantry were not following, and they were being mown down.

At last we had got the tanks going forward again. Bullets were still crackling all around. My throat was dry with excitement and shouting. I sought a momentary refuge in the ditch where I drained my water-bottle and whisky flask at a gulp. There flashed into my mind the picture of an old native woman in the Argentine whom my mother had taken me to visit. Her next-door neighbour was in the habit of firing off a rifle when he was in a bad temper. He was in one of these moods that afternoon and had let off several shots. The old woman, always in fear that a stray bullet would come through her window, immediately had rushed to a bottle of cognac . . . Suddenly, I heard the muttering voices of men creeping towards me along the ditch. They were Australians advancing in crouching position, with fixed bayonets. The first man hissing: "Who are you?" was about to stick his bayonet in me, when I hastily replied: "Tanks!"

I was on the road again with the tanks, when I heard a shout, and turning, found the adjutant of the infantry four of five yards away. He told me that the Colonel had been killed and that the infantry had suffered such severe casualties that they were retiring in extended order. I said the tanks were going forward to continue the attack. He declared that the infantry were so disorganized that it would be impossible for them to follow. He has since explained that he *discovered that the scout officer and the leading company commander had both been seriously wounded, and that there was no one else who knew the route.*

*I then went back to tell the commanding officer, but when I arrived at the place I had left him found that he had just been killed. I then found the next senior officer in the battalion and told him he was in command.*

*As there was now no one left in the battalion who knew the route he decided it was useless to go on.*

I was not told at the time that this was the predicament. If I had been I should have said that I knew the way for I certainly thought so; although, as far as I remember, there was only one map with route picked out on it and that was in the possession of Lieut. McNicol, the Reconnaissance Officer.

The thought had crossed my mind: "What would the rest of the operation be like, since just at the start all my tank crews were wounded and depleted!" Now, without infantry support, I decided it would be useless for the tanks to advance further and I gave the order to retire. Again, I had the same difficulty turning them. I felt rather like a wild animal tamer with huge beasts to control. In the dark the tank crews could not easily understand my directions nor hear my voice above the noise. Every time the tanks moved the enemy machine-guns simply went mad, and there was a terrific fusillade of bullets.

The tanks had moved back about one-hundred-and-fifty yards when I found a revolver being brandished in my face. Replying to the challenge, I found I was being mistaken for one of the enemy by an Australian officer at the head of the second battalion of infantry, which had apparently come up. He seemed to be in a state of frenzy! So great was the noise of the firing together with the clatter of my own tanks on the road that I had not heard the approach of the reserve tanks and infantry, nor could I see them in the dark. I ordered the tanks to halt while I explained to him what had happened, and, while we were deciding what to do, Grounds appeared from the rear, having evidently come up with the reserves.

We now held a conference, all standing in the middle of the road. I thought how damn' silly it was, for bullets were still whizzing close by, and each time we jerked our heads instinctively. It would have been safer to take cover in the ditch; but I realized that not one of us was going to be the first to make the move. So, while we talked, we stuck our ground as though such things as bullets didn't exist. Grounds said: "We'll do whatever you want. I can order the tanks forward, but look at the state of the crews!"

I wondered if the reserves would be pushed through at once to carry on with the good work. Not so, however! The commanding officer of the reserve battalion decided he would await orders from the Brigade Commander, and Grounds went back immediately to explain the position to him. Meanwhile, until I received fresh instructions, I was to keep my tanks where they were, motionless and silent, so as not to draw the enemy fire.

Jones was a warm-hearted Welshman. He had come up in command of the reserve tanks and expected to find us all dead. In his relief at finding me alive, he flung his arm round my neck in a warm embrace. We sheltered sometimes between the horns of a tank and sometimes inside one. I was glad of his company for I was feeling dazed. It must have been now about two hours since the first bomb had dropped and all this time I had been under heavy fire. Curiously enough, the shelling which had commenced when the enemy detected the attack had stopped pretty soon. Probably in the darkness his shells were doing damage to his own troops and for that reason his artillery bombardment had been discontinued.

It turned out that I was not the only tank officer who was held up at the point of a revolver by an Australian. This had, also, happened to Humphreys, who had been told: "If you value your life, the tanks will not move." Apropos of the present account, Stittle, my runner, wrote me: *As I read the narrative everything came back to my mind as though it were a recent happening. Every detail you record is only too true and I marvel that after all these years you have been able to give such a vivid description. I was not previously aware that you had been challenged at the point of the revolver on that delightful evening. A similar experience came my way. When we went forward to turn the tanks back into action, I happened to be standing in front of the leading tank when along comes an Australian officer brandishing his revolver and threatening me with my life if the tanks so much as moved. I explained who I was but it made no difference. He said: "I put you in charge and if these tanks move you will be shot." His point was that we were drawing the enemy fire. I often wonder if he ever returned to cover as, no sooner had he left me than it started to rain bullets all round, and turning one side of the tank in front of which I was standing into a glorified pepper-box. Once the fire had died down I, of course, returned to you.*

In a tense silence the six tanks and the supporting infantry waited, expecting that at any moment the enemy might counter-attack.

After what seemed an interminable time, during which we were behind the enemy lines, a runner came with the message that the tanks were to remain silent so that the infantry could retire in safety. We were to stay put until we received word from the infantry that they had withdrawn.

We remained out in front for another hour-and-a-half, covering their retirement. All the time we were on the qui-vive in case the enemy should surround us. Owing to the darkness, concerted action by the tanks would be impossible, and we should be in a predicament without infantry support.

At last a runner reported: "All clear!"

A hail of bullets sped the departing tanks, as at three-forty-five in the morning, they took leave of the enemy after spending five-and-a-half hours in his company. I travelled back inside one of the tanks. Rumbling along the main road we passed the Headquarters of the 10th Australian Infantry Brigade in a dug-out close by. We were stopped there and a message was delivered that the Infantry General wished to speak to "O.C. Tanks."

I was taken to him. There were other Staff Officers present. It was a formal interview. The General spoke in a very serious tone, and wished me to make a statement of exactly what had happened. He told me that the Reconnaissance Officer at the head of the 37th Battalion had been wounded in the foot, and on his way to the Casualty Clearing Station had been brought to him to give an account of the operation. He impressed upon me that he was a man noted for his veracity. I related the whole story, omitting nothing and explaining how the noise of the tanks had drawn the fire of the enemy, not only on themselves, but also on the infantry who were doing their best to keep in close touch. Regretfully I agreed that the presence of tanks in the dark had been a hindrance to the infantry instead of a help.

The General thanked me for my statement. With a feeling of relief I heard that it coincided in every detail with what the Reconnaissance Officer had said. The General admitted that he could see now that it had been a great mistake to use tanks at all in the operation. With great sorrow, he told me that in it he had lost a very fine Battalion Commander, and of a magnificent battalion of one-thousand men who had gone into action, only one-hundred had come through.

> " Come thro' the jaws of Death,
> Back from the mouth of Hell,
> All that was left of them,
> Left of (*ten*) hundred."

Humphreys was very badly shaken by his experience of that night, and had collapsed at the First Field Dressing Station in a cellar. Two days later he crossed to England on the same hospital ship as the Reconnaissance Officer. The latter had been wounded when riding on the back of Jefferies' tank. On board ship he was writing up his report and tried to get as much information as he could from Humphreys. He wanted to know why the tanks had turned. Humphreys replied that

[*Imperial War Museum*

(*Above*) MODEL INTERIOR OF MARK V TANK
(*Below*) SCENE OF NIGHT ATTACK
Amiens—St. Quentin Road, looking towards La Flaque from spot
where action took place. The buildings in the background are at La
Flaque. In August, 1918, the road was lined with hedges and trees.
Photo taken in September, 1924

the tanks had very definite orders to keep in close touch with the infantry and as the latter were nowhere to be seen the tanks had turned to find them.

It so happened that Glanville came across in hospital an Australian officer who had been wounded in this action. The fellow was suffering from a wound which would not heal, and he was weak from continual loss of blood. He told Glanville that he had been in several stiff fights, but none of them had been so terrible as that night attack with tanks.

The following is an account of the Proyart action as described by Captain W. J. Denny, M.C., M.P., in his article on the work of the Australians, published in the *Daily Telegraph* of the 1st April 1919.

*Owing to the disadvantage of having the Valley of the Somme as an inter-corps boundary, the Australian Corps Commander prevailed upon the Army authorities to permit him to extend his battle front northwards so as to enable him to get astride of the Somme Valley. This disposition had a most important bearing upon subsequent events. The 3rd and 4th Divisions were ordered to carry out an encircling operation on the night of August 10-11 in order to cut off the Etinhem spur north of the Somme and the ridge east of Proyart, south of the Somme. The general lines of the operation both to the north and the south of the river were similar. Columns were to move along defined roads leaving the objectives well to the flanks and then encircle the enemy positions. Each column was accompanied by tanks, and was to move in an easterly direction and then to wheel inwards towards the Somme. It was recognized that this action involved certain risks as tanks had never been tried by night in this way, but in view of the condition of the enemy's morale at this stage it was considered that the effect of the advance of the tanks and infantry would lead immediately to the collapse of the defence. The action north of the river was entirely successful. South of the river the enemy bombed the forward area heavily early in the night on the 3rd Division front, causing considerable delay in the preparations for the attack. The progress on the southern sector was at first slow owing to heavy enemy artillery and machine-gun fire and the disorganization caused by the bombing. Two of the tanks allotted for the operations were destroyed or put out of action very soon after zero hour.* **Heavy casualties having been suffered by units of the 10th Infantry Brigade,** *it was decided that this brigade, as it was unable to carry out that operation as ordered, should co-operate with the 9th Infantry Brigade by taking up a position round the eastern outskirts of Proyart.* **The 9th Brigade was to complete the capture of Provart.**

The black italics are mine to emphasise the "heavy casualties" of the 10th Infantry Brigade which was in the night attack.

This account states that "the general lines of the operation both to the north and south of the river were similar." Actually, there was a very important difference. By studying the map, it is evident that the attack north of the Somme followed a comparatively unimportant road; while the attack on the south was along a Route

Nationale—a principal high road of France. The two routes could not be compared. They were as dissimilar as the Great North Road in England is to a country lane. It should have been obvious that the defence of such an important Route Nationale would be exceptionally strong. . . .

My interview with the Australian Infantry Brigadier finished, I walked alone down the main road to Bayonvillers, the tanks having already returned. I reached the village at dawn.

## V

August the 10th had been an unlucky day for tanks. The eighty-five which had gone into action had suffered heavily in every sector. Of the forty-three which went in with the Canadians, twenty-three received direct hits. Only too true were the words of Ludendorff in a secret Order of August the 11th, "A tank is an easy prey for artillery of all calibres."

After a massed attack reverses in subsequent sideshows with tanks were only to be expected. These sideshows were usually expensive and fruitless. It puzzled me why tanks were wasted in them instead of being kept for another pitched battle. The proper use of tanks, it seemed to me, was in swarms where they were not expected.

My return to Bayonvillers had been at dawn on the morning of Sunday, the 11th. My first thought was to get rest. I found, however, that I could not sleep for long owing to my exhausted state. In the shelter of the hedge where the tanks were camouflaged, I sat down to prepare my report, which had been called for. My head was reeling, and I could scarcely collect my thoughts. With Glanville's help I composed my report and the recommendations; but I was so badly shaken that I could not write them myself, and they had to be copied out for me. I thought a report should be as short and restrained as possible, and mine was certainly neither long nor florid.

Just before 10 o'clock the following morning, the 12th, my report and recommendations, written "In the Field," were handed in. That day our Tank Brigade, having been fought to a standstill, was withdrawn. My section, after being twice in action, had been badly knocked about. Out of the total number of twenty-two who had been in the fighting—there had been a replacement for Corporal Dunn—only four or five were unwounded.

Our Company went back to Blangy Château Camp in the valley of the Somme, near Blangy Tronville, where the third company of the battalion had been stationed while we were at Tronville Wood.

The results of the Battle of Amiens (8th-12th August) are described in Sir Douglas Haig's Victory Dispatch: *Within the space of five days the town of Amiens and the railway centring upon it had been disengaged. . . . Nearly 22,000 prisoners and over four hundred guns had been taken by us, and our line had been pushed forward to a depth of some twelve miles in a vital sector. Further, our deep advance, combined with the attacks of the French Armies on our right had compelled the enemy to evacuate hurriedly a wide extent of territory to the south of us. The effort of this victory, following so closely after the allied victory on the Marne, upon the morale both of the German and British troops was very great. Buoyed up by the hope of immediate and decisive victory to be followed by an early and favourable peace, constantly assured that the allied reserves were exhausted, the German soldiery suddenly found themselves attacked on two fronts and thrown back with heavy losses from large and important portions of their earlier gains. The reaction was inevitable and of a deep and lasting character. On the other hand, our own troops felt that at last their opportunity had come, and that, supported by a superior artillery and numerous tanks, they could now press forward resolutely to reap the reward of their patient, dauntless, and successful defence in* March *and* April.

## 6

Our camp was situated in the grounds of Blangy Château in an angle formed by a road and the Amiens-Nesle railway line. I had a bell-tent in amongst the trees close to the road which went through the grounds and under the railway embankment.

I was in a state of utter nervous collapse and lay in my tent, unable to sleep, my mind whirling round all the time. I do not think that the others realized how bad I felt. After smoking a pipe, I shook all over, and had finally had to give it up altogether. A form of exercise which I enjoyed was quoit-tennis. A rope had been fixed up between two trees, where there was sufficient space. After the

dry summer the earth was hard and had an easy
surface to play on. The game was splendid exercise,
and it took my thoughts off the nightmare of that
ghastly holocaust.

Monday, the 5th, had been August Bank Holiday.
My father had returned home that day from a long
week-end in the Shakespeare country. My mother
returned from Llandrindod Wells on the Thursday,
the 8th, the day of the big massed attack east of
Amiens. They were, therefore, back just in time to
get the full blast of the screaming headlines of
the London newspapers—JOINT ATTACK BY
BRITISH AND FRENCH—ENEMY SUR-
PRISED BY SUDDEN ASSAULT—ADVANCE
IN A MIST—ALLIES' INITIATIVE—WORK
OF THE TANKS—TREMENDOUS DRUM-
FIRE. One paper announced on Friday morning:
"The good news from the front was made known
in a number of London theatres last night, and was
everywhere received with great enthusiasm." This
kind of gratifying intelligence no longer cheered my
father and mother, for the word "Tanks" had only
to be mentioned in such an announcement and they
feared the worst.

On Friday, the 16th, the tanks which had been
engaged in the battle were inspected by Sir Douglas
Haig. The inspection took place in the actual
battlefield. This was the first time the tanks had
been complimented by a personal visit of the Commander-in-Chief after an action. I thought he
looked very old and worried. An amazing change
had been wrought in the attitude of the High Command towards tanks. When I had arrived in
France they were on the point of being scrapped as

utterly useless. Now, a year later, after they had been properly used, their value in action was appreciated. In his Victory Dispatch, Sir Douglas Haig paid tribute to them! The following are his words: *The whole scheme of the attack of 8th August was dependent upon tanks. . . . So great has been the effect produced upon the German infantry by the appearance of British tanks that in more than one instance when for various reasons real tanks were not available in sufficient numbers, valuable results have been obtained by the use of dummy tanks painted on frames of wood and canvas. It is no disparagement of the courage of our infantry or of the skill and devotion of our artillery, to say that the achievements of those essential arms would have fallen short of the full measure of success achieved by our Armies had it not been for the very gallant and devoted work of the Tank Corps, under the command of Major-General H. J. Elles."*

General von Zwehl in 1921 said: "It was not the genius of Marshal Foch that defeated us, but 'General Tank.' "

Major-General J. F. C. Fuller, who was the first Chief of Staff of the Tank Corps, in his book *War and Western Civilization 1832-1932*, refers to Colonel C. B. Brackenbury and his article in *The Nineteenth-Century Review* entitled "Iron-clad Field Artillery," written in July 1878. General Fuller quotes from the article:

" 'The fire of infantry has become so formidable of late years that defensive measures must inevitably be adopted sooner or later by field artillery. . . . If . . . we add the use of defensive armour which can be carried by artillery and

R

cannot be carried by cavalry and infantry, a power will be created which must seriously modify the tactics of the battlefield. The development is as sure to come as the day to follow the night. We may hope that England will set the example instead of following other nations.' "

General Fuller goes on:

"This idea was realized by the English on September the 15th 1916, when tanks advanced over the battlefield of the Somme. Brackenbury saw clearly that 'Moral effect is the object aimed at in a battle, for the killed and wounded have no influence on the final retirement.' He saw, as Frederick the Great had seen, 'that to advance is to conquer,' because of the terrifying moral effect of a *continuous* advance. This was the underlying idea of the 'bayonet school' of military thought, an idea pre-eminently sound, but in the circumstances impossible. The 'shell school' of 1914-1917 never grasped this idea; it could not, or did not, see that the problem was not to reduce the enemy's position to mud and rubble but *to advance the guns* under hostile rifle and machine-gun fire; and that, could such an advance be made it would prove *not overwhelmingly destructive but overwhelmingly demoralizing.* This is exactly what the tank— mobile armoured artillery—accomplished and proved.

"On the first day (July 1) of the Battle of the Somme in 1916, a battle fought according to the doctrines of the 'shell school,' British casualties numbered close upon 60,000. On the first day (August 8) of the Battle of Amiens in 1918, the most decisive battle of the War, a battle fought according to the doctrines of the 'tank school,' British casualties were slightly under 1,000 and the Germans captured exceeded the numbers of Germans killed by thousands.

"During July, August, September, October and November 1916, the British Army lost approximately 475,000 men, it captured 30,000 prisoners and occupied some 90 square miles of country. During the same months in 1917 the losses were 370,000, the prisoners captured were 25,000, and the ground occupied was about 45 square miles. In July, August, September, October and November 1918, the losses were 345,000, the prisoners captured 176,000, and the ground occupied was 4,000 square miles. If now we divide these losses by the number of square miles captured we shall obtain a rough estimate of casualties per square mile gained. These figures are approximately as follows:

(a)      July to November 1916:
    475,000 ÷ 90 sq. miles = 5,277 casualties per sq. mile.
(b)      July to November 1917:
    370,000 ÷ 45 sq. miles = 8,222 casualties per sq. mile.
(c)      July to November 1918:
    345,000 ÷ 4,000 sq. miles = 86 casualties per sq. mile.

"In the third period alone were tanks used efficiently." (From *The Reformation of War* by Colonel J. F. C. Fuller.)

"The 'tank school,' the brain of which was the Tank Corps General Staff, never ceased to think in terms of the moral attack; not because they were kindly disposed to the enemy but because they realized that this was the most economical and decisive form of attack. In 1917 they suggested carrying machine-gunners in large tanks *through* the enemy's battle front and depositing them in rear of it. Why? Because the rear is the *morally weakest point* in the enemy's battle body. In 1918 they again suggested passing high-speed tanks through the enemy's battle front and attacking the enemy's command headquarters in rear. Why? Because a shot through the brain paralyses the body and leads to a *moral debâcle*. This suggestion was accepted by Marshal Foch as the basic idea of his 1919 plan of campaign.

"Then came the armistice and back came the 'bayonet school' into its own. In the 1924 edition of the British *Field Service Regulations* we read: 'Infantry is the arm which in the end wins battles. . . . The rifle and the bayonet are the infantryman's chief weapons. The battle can be won in the last resort only by means of these weapons.' "

.     .     .     .     .

August the 22nd was the anniversary of my arrival in France, and now I put up my second chevron to which I was entitled after a year's active service with the British Expeditionary Force.

From now on until the end of the month, I seem to have lost track of dates; but I believe it was about August the 28th that the company was preparing to entrain at Villers-Bretonneux to go to another part of the line. Then unexpectedly I got

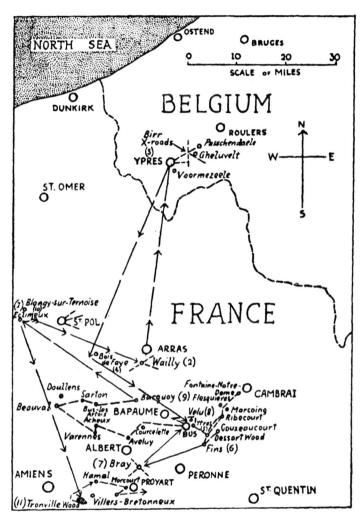

JOURNEYS OF THE TANKS

orders to return to England. New battalions were being formed, and personnel of old battalions were to be the nuclei of the new units. I had only two hours' notice, but no more was necessary. My kit was already packed—it had been for days—and I did not require to be told to hurry. I was sorry to say good-bye to my Section, and to Kydd, who had been my devoted and faithful batman since the beginning of 1917; but I was not sorry to be going to England for a while.

As I made my way to England, still an "Acting Captain," my thoughts went back over the last year during which I had had so many thrilling experiences and had helped to make history.

I remembered my first experience of shellfire at Wailly, when the cook-house had gone up into the air, and our battalion had suffered its first casualty. Unpleasant as this occurrence had been, it had paled into insignificance before the events of the first day in the Ypres Salient, when Gerrard and I had ploughed our way across miles of mud, among the massed guns and had twice been caught in the enemy's barrage.

Then there rose before my mind the melancholy vision of the burial by night at Voormezeele of the men who had been killed at the tanks near Birr X-Rd.

I saw Gerrard's face again when he returned to the dug-out after hearing that he was to attack Polderhoek Chateau, the next dawn but one; and then my own experience that morning trying to mend the Ypres-Menin road in the midst of a double barrage, and my hectic search for "A's" lost party.

Then followed one of the red-letter days of the War, the 20th November 1917, when the success of the tanks at the commencement of the battle of Cambrai electrified the world and set the bells of St. Paul's pealing. I was proud that my Section had been in the centre of this all-important battle, which had taught us how the War could be won. Even more thrilling for me was the next day, when we attacked and captured Fontaine-Notre-Dame! The numb horror of those minutes during which our tank was stuck on the ridge with the enemy guns blazing at us, and we thought each moment would be our last. And the feeling of excited relief when we got going again and charged down the slope, and the enemy ceased firing. I remembered with pride that the taking of this village by my Section and Viveash's tank "Hong Kong", had constituted the culminating point of the advance on Cambrai! Then came the difficult and dangerous trek back in the darkness, when we did not know where we were going, and I had walked outside the tanks with Hughes. The sudden alarm when we saw the figures in the sunken road, and the relief at finding they were not the enemy. Eventually, we had arrived at Cantaing, and there had followed my chance meeting with Rowbotham, whom I had not seen for ten years. Finally, the joy of Spray's welcome, when he had guided me to the dug-out at La Justice, where Pearson was stretched out with a heart attack.

Another memory was of listening-in at the La Justice dug-out, to the attack of the Highland Division and the forty tanks in an attempt to recapture Fontaine. Later, when we were at Fins, had come the German counter-offensive at Gouzeau-court. I had been Second-in-Command of the nineteen tanks which had charged Gauche Wood. The work of this Composite Company had been mentioned by Sir Douglas Haig in his dispatch.

After our rest in winter quarters had come the March Retreat—the first strategic withdrawal in which tanks had fought a deliberate rearguard action—the shock and confusion of the 21st March. Three days later, on the 24th March (my birthday), I had been on the extreme right of the Third Army at the now historic gap where the Third and Fifth Armies had lost touch with disastrous results. There we had counter-attacked at Bus, and helped the Second Division to get away. General Pereira, commanding that division, had thanked us. I remembered the sickening numbness I had felt when I saw the man escaping from Bus, shot through the head only a few yards away as he approached me. That same day as we covered the retreating Third Army, just before crossing the road at Le Transloy, the enemy plane, like an angry wasp, had swooped down on my one remaining tank and machine-gunned it. I thought of my dive into a shell-hole, wishing I had the characteristic accomplishment of the chameleon. In imagination I went again up to the line at Bucquoy, and along the mud-logged trench with shells bursting on the edges above us.

Then had followed three consecutive periods of responsibility, less thrilling, but important. I had been in command of the tank defences of St. Pol during a critical time. Again, when there was a certain anxiety, I had been in charge of the two forward tanks at Villers-Bretonneux, which would bear the brunt of the expected grand-scale attack of the enemy's tank corps. I was not even allowed to have my rest in peace, for lest I withered by inaction, I had been placed in command of the Officers' Company at the Tank Corps Base.

Next my mind reverted to recent events—the battle of Amiens—the plan of which had been modelled on the epoch-making battle of Cambrai. My helplessness in the mist, and the dread of not being in my place in time; the burial of the Australian—it had not been a pleasant memory to take with me into action. Then on the ridge beyond Morcourt, with the gun firing across the Somme at the tank, and my narrow escape from death. Then Viveash's death the next day on the same ridge at practically the same place.

I did not want to recall the events of the night of the 10th/11th August, but they rose overwhelmingly before my mind. Again, I had had the doubtful honour of being chosen to take part in a difficult and hazardous operation—the first organized night attack with tanks! The apprehension when we saw the Boche plane overhead in the afternoon during our *daylight approach march!* What hell would await us if we had been spotted? The suspense at La Flaque when nothing happened. The crash of the first bomb—the din of further bombs, shells and machine-gun bullets. The clatter of the tanks and the noise from their guns! The savage crack of bullets hissing through the air! I tried to shut the scene out of my mind, but it was useless. I saw again the road raked by machine-gun bullets and the lurid light of the flares; the advancing men falling like corn at the reaping and Colonel Knox-Knight shot dead at my side. The nightmare of turning the tanks, and the frenzied Australian who threatened to shoot me, pointing his revolver in my face with his finger on the trigger. Then, while I was still dazed by the events of the preceding hours, had come my interview with the Australian General. He had not been hostile to me after hearing my detailed account; but in the state of mind I was in, I felt that since the attack had been a failure as far as the tanks were concerned, I would be made the scapegoat, if one were wanted, for the disaster. During the critical and dangerous part of the attack I had had the sole responsibility of the tanks. Moreover, after the couple of minutes of the conference, I had not seen Grounds again that night. I had been again the senior officer responsible on the spot.

I was going back to England after twelve months in France and Belgium, during which I had been in the Ypres Salient and had fought with the tanks over most of the forty-five miles between Cambrai and Amiens. I had taken part in all the big tank battles.

# CHAPTER X

# ENGLAND.
## THE ARMISTICE AND AFTERWARDS

### I

I WENT straight home on my arrival in England. It was the 30th of August, and the day was a Friday. On the Sunday I reported at the depôt at Wareham. There I had to spend three monotonous days. I thought this camp of wooden huts the dreariest and most inhospitable place I had been in.

My overdue leave eventually came through on Tuesday, the 3rd September.

On my reporting at Bovington on Tuesday, the 17th September, I was posted to the 20th Tank Battalion—one of the new battalions being formed there. The camp had now assumed a more cheerful aspect, partly due to the presence of so many pretty W.A.A.C.s, and also to a garrison theatre.

On the morning of the 5th of October we heard from France. Our old battalion had been in again and suffered severely. Glanville won a bar to his M.C. At a much later date, he told me of an incident in this attack, which he thought was better worth the M.C. than the service for which he had got it. The infantry had gone through a village without "mopping up" the dug-outs and cellars. Glanville and a number of men were on a road, when an N.C.O.

gunner, pointing out to one side where there was evidently a dug-out full of Germans, shouted: "Come on, you fellows! Who will follow me? Let's clear them out." No one seemed very anxious to move. Glanville, as an officer, thought he had better take the lead and called out: "Yes, come on!" and started off himself. When half-way there, he was horrified to find that no one had followed him. Pride forbade him to turn back. His mind worked quickly. Shouting orders to an imaginary party of men (as though they were concealed from the enemy) he marched on to the dug-out. Still shouting instructions, "Party, right turn. Halt. Mark-time. Quick march," and so on, and covering the Germans in the dug-out with his revolver, he made them come out one by one— some twenty of them—and surrender, depositing their arms in a little pile in front of him!

About this time I was appointed Second-in-Command of the Company.

Towards the end of October I learned that the decorations were out for the battle of Amiens. Grounds had got a bar to his D.S.O., as I later learned for the night attack. No officer of my Section had got even a "mention". Neal and Stittle had each got a well-earned D.C.M. and had been promoted Sergeant from the ranks, Stittle afterwards becoming a Company-Sergeant-Major. Sergeant Mitchell, who had been in "Hadrian" at Cambrai and who had been transferred from my Section just before the battle of Amiens, had received the D.C.M. in recognition of his achievement when acting as an N.C.O. tank commander in the attack against Morcourt on the 8th August.

Then came the Armistice. I thought "thank heaven the War is over! Now for the future!" We celebrated the occasion that night. Everybody went mad. The Regimental-Sergeant-Major, dressed as a W.A.A.C., served in the Mess at dinner. At an early hour a good many were blind. The following day I was put in charge of a picket formed to quell any disturbance likely to endanger the safety of the camp.

2

Demobilization started immediately.

My application to be demobilized went through quickly, and on the 3rd of January 1919, I passed through the Dispersal Centre at Wimbledon, still as an "acting captain" and "disembodied" in more senses than one.

Towards the end of the month I received a stereotyped letter from the Secretary to the Army Council, ratifying my demobilization, and concluding with the words:

*I am also to take this opportunity of conveying the thanks of the Army Council for your services to the country during the late War, and for the excellent work you have done.*

Glad as I was of this appreciation, I should have valued more a few personal "remarks" in my "Officer's Record of Services. Army Book 439." The page where any achievement or duty well carried out might be recorded, still remained a blank. No Commanding Officer, or General Officer under whom I had served overseas, had asked me for my Record of Services Book, to "state" there "in his own handwriting" how I had acquitted myself in even one of the many difficult, important and hazardous operations which had fallen to my lot with the tanks in France and Flanders.

On the 8th of February 1919, there was the following announcement in the *London Gazette*:

*War Office. Feb. 8th. Regular Forces. Tank Corps. Lieut. (acting Capt.) to be temp. Capt. D. E. Hickey (Suff. R., T.F.) (Oct. 19th* 1918).

The pity was I did not get my *temporary rank* until after I was out of the Army.

. . . . .

My gratuity, in due course, came through, and amounted to £209 5s.

# APPENDICES

# APPENDICES

## I. BATTLE OF CAMBRAI
### REPORTS OF THREE TANK COMMANDERS
### CAPTAIN HICKEY'S REPORT
### G.H.Q. OFFICIAL COMMUNIQUÉ

### I. BATTLE OF CAMBRAI
#### REPORTS OF THREE TANK COMMANDERS

From: 2/Lieut. G. Dudley Hardy,
    O.C. "Hadrian", Crew No. 28,
        No. 7 Section, 23 Coy., H. Battn.
To: O.C. No. 7 Sect., 23 Coy.,
    H. Battn.

                                     22/11/17.

Sir,

    With reference to the actions of Tuesday, 20/11/17, and Wednesday, 21/11/17, I have the honour to report as follows:

*Tuesday*, 20/11/17.          *Map Ref. Marcoing* 1/10,000.

6.10 a.m.    Left. Coy. Point of Assembly; south of Beaucamp.

6.50 a.m.    Crossed Starting Line 100 x East of Argyle Road. The first two waves of Ospreys were well ahead with their infantry. As we crossed our own Front Line we were subjected to accurate hostile gunfire —possibly direct laying. Casualties among the infantry were very few.

7.15 a.m.    Crossed own Front Line.

7.25 a.m.    Crossed Plush Trench.

7.34 a.m.    Crossed Hindenburg Line without difficulty behind "Hermit".

8.8 a.m.    Crossed Support Line behind "Helen". Both crossings of Hindenburg Line were easily accomplished on fascines previously dropped by other Ospreys.

8.15 a.m.    Crossed Mole Trench.

9.30 a.m.    Fired first shot on outskirts of Ribécourt. Sent pigeon message.

| 9.40 a.m. | Crossed Blue Line. |
| 9.43 a.m. | In descending a steep bank on to a light railway east of the railway, the fascine broke loose at the back and fell. |
| 9.55 a.m. | Crossed railway at Marcoing 1/10,000 L.20.d.4.3. Sent Signal "Assume Battle Formation". |
| 10.00 a.m. | Reached Objective (Area 10) but found the trenches unoccupied and no opposition. Other Ospreys were going forward; no hostile infantry; no hostile artillery. |
| 10.15 a.m. | Opened fire with 6-pdrs. on Farm (Niergnies. Ed. 1. Special Sheet 21.d.45.85.). After about six rounds one German Officer and about twenty other ranks were observed to run out and were successfully dealt with by our machine-guns. |
| 10.35 a.m. | Reached the outskirts of Marcoing. No enemy resistance; no hostile artillery. Sent signal "Return to Rallying Point". |
| 10.45 a.m. | Sent second pigeon message. |
| 12.30 p.m. | Reached Rallying Point. Camouflaged and greased up. |

*Report (Map Ref. Niergnies 1/20,000) on Action of Wednesday, 21/11/17.*

| 11.30 a.m. | Started up and left Rallying Point behind "Harlequin". |
| 1.45 p.m. | Left vicinity of Beetroot Factory L.13.c.5.8. and proceeded in line with 200 x interval between Ospreys, leaving Orival Wood on our left. |
| 2.45 p.m. | Opened fire on Cantaing Mill, which was holding up our infantry. After a few rounds from 6-pdr. and Lewis guns, the infantry were able to advance. |
| 3.00 p.m. | Proceeded towards Cantaing, which the infantry reported to contain hostile machine-guns and snipers. Observed Osprey B20 on fire in Cantaing-Fontaine sunken road. After working round southern edge of village the infantry was able to advance, though they reported lack of ammunition. We then proceeded towards our objective—Fontaine. |
| 4.00 p.m. | While crossing the ridge on the way to Fontaine we were subjected to very heavy direct laying gun-fire of about four-inch calibre. I observed the |

flashes of a hostile battery situated in the vicinity of F.14 Central, and directed my gunners to open fire upon it, and after a few rounds, as far as we could judge, the battery was silenced. The Osprey "Hong-Kong", which was the first to be fired upon by this battery, had a miraculous escape, shells falling so close that she appeared to be hit about a dozen times. We ourselves escaped only by zig-zagging off our course every time our position was registered by the battery. Having crossed the ridge we proceeded in fourth speed down the valley to the village.

4.30 p.m.   Reached Fontaine and worked round the southern edge. No hostile infantry in sight; our own infantry following at considerable distance. As it was now dark with a heavy ground mist, and we were very short of ammunition and other supplies, the O.C. Section in conference with Tank Commanders, decided to return as soon as our own infantry should have entered the village, which was now free from the enemy.

5.00 p.m.   Our own infantry having entered the village, we started on the return journey along the Fontaine-Cantaing sunken road. On reaching Cantaing found radiator leaking and petrol running short, but managed to continue on our iron ration of petrol and water.

9.00 p.m.   Reached Rallying Point.

### General Note.

*Autovac.*   Throughout the two days the Autovac gave continual trouble and proved highly unsatisfactory.

*Lewis Guns.*   On the second day the Lewis guns were constantly having stoppages—nearly all number threes.

*Radiator.*   The leak in the radiator was probably caused by bumping in and out of the many sunken roads.

*Spuds.*   Spuds were very much damaged by the hard roads.

*Secondary Gears.*   Gears are very worn and gear-changing difficult.

*Supplies.*   The engine oil supplied (Mobiloil A) was far too thin for the work.

*Tracks.*   Tracks require shortening.

*Fascine.* The fascine as a means of crossing the Hindenburg Line was very successful, but the method of securing it to the top of the Osprey is not sufficiently strong.

Throughout the two actions the crew behaved splendidly. My driver, L/Cpl. Dunn, drove throughout and acted with great coolness and good judgment. He drove for eight hours on the first day and ten hours on the second day.

I have the honour to be, Sir,

Your obedient servant,

G. DUDLEY HARDY, 2nd/Lieut.

O.C. "Hadrian".

From: 2/Lieut. K. E. Hughes,
O.C. "Havoc," Crew No. 27,
To: O.C. No. 7 Sect., 23 Coy., H. Battn.

22/xi/17.

Sir,

I have the honour to report with regard to the actions of 20/xi/17 and 21/xi/17 as follows:

*Action of 20/xi/17.*                    *Ref.* 1/10,000 *Marcoing.*

| | |
|---|---|
| 6.10 a.m. | Left Coy. point of assembly S. of Beaucamp. |
| 6.50 a.m. | Crossed starting line. First two waves with their infantry being well in advance. |
| 6.55 a.m. | Broke and repaired fan belt. |
| 7.5 a.m. | Crossed Village Support at Q.12.b.3.9. and came under heavy shell fire probably direct laying. |
| 7.10 a.m. | Saw unknown Osprey ditched at about Q.6.b.5.5. |
| 7.15 a.m. | Crossed Village Trench and picked up infantry. |
| 7.31 a.m. | Crossed Plush Trench at Q.6.b.7.2. |
| 7.48 a.m. | Crossed Valley Trench. |
| 7.50 a.m. | Held up owing to congestion of the previous waves. |
| 8.25 a.m. | Received shutter message from "Hermosa", "Waiting for infantry on right to come up." |
| 8.40 a.m. | Infantry in position. |
| 8.46 a.m. | Crossed Valley Support. |
| 8.50 a.m. | Crossed Mob Trench. |
| 8.55 a.m. | Saw unknown Osprey burning about L.31.c.5.9. |
| 9.30 a.m. | Passed through S.E. corner of Ribécourt. |
| 9.50 a.m. | Crossed Blue Line. |
| 10.10 a.m. | Crossed railway at L.20.d.4.3. |
| 10.15 a.m. | Reached objective (Area 10) and encountered no opposition, so proceeded towards Marcoing. |

| | |
|---|---|
| 10.20 a.m. | Fascine chain broke while descending steep slope. |
| 10.35 a.m. | Opened fire on house at L.21.d.45.85 and observed hostile infantry attempting to escape. |
| 10.45 a.m. | Fired on house at L.21.d.75.79 and secured direct hits. |
| 11.00 a.m. | Reached W. side of Marcoing. |
| 11.15 a.m. | Received disc message transmitted by "Hermosa", to return to rally point. |
| 11.30 a.m. | Unditching-boom "U" bolts broke and boom fell. |
| 11.31 a.m. | Saw German enter dug-out near L.21.d.45.85; so with 78486 L/Cpl. Stanton I entered the dug-out and captured five prisoners, some arms and S.A.A., which I handed over to infantry. |
| 11.45 a.m. | Captured four more prisoners who were attempting to escape in direction of Marcoing and handed these to infantry, who had reached us by this time. |
| 12.00 noon. | Captured German Officer. |
| 12.5 p.m. | Repairs to boom completed, though we were being continually sniped from Marcoing Wood, and with "Hermosa" made for rallying point. |
| 12.30. p.m. | Came under heavy artillery fire in neighbourhood of L.21.c. |
| 1.5 p.m. | Reached rallying point at L.20.d.8.3., near which a flare dump was burning. |

*Report on action of* 21/11/17.　　*Ref.* 1/10,000 *Niergnies.*

| | |
|---|---|
| 11.30 a.m. | Left Coy. rallying point behind No. 5 Section and proceeded N.W. in direction of Flesquieres. |
| 1.10 p.m. | Reached Beetroot Factory at L.13.c.5.8. and received orders from O.C. 23 Coy. to attack Fontaine-Notre-Dame. |
| 1.30 p.m. | Passed Orival Wood on our left, the section being in line, Ospreys at 200 x interval. |
| 1.50 p.m. | Passed La Justice. |
| 2.00 p.m. | Passed through infantry, who stated that their front line was in neighbourhood of L.22 and that they were being held up by fire from Cantaing Mill. |
| 2.45 p.m. | Opened fire on Cantaing Mill and on the trench system on either side of it and cleared them. |
| 3.00 p.m. | Opened fire on Cantaing, from which our infantry were retiring, and put them in possession of it. Lewis gun fire kept up on retreating hostile infantry. |

| | |
|---|---|
| 3.15 p.m. | Saw Male Osprey B.20 on fire in sunken road at B.20.d.8.1 (approx.). |
| 3.25 p.m. | Saw our infantry retiring from Fontaine and opened heavy 6-pdr. and Lewis gun fire on village. Proceeded towards E. corner of village. |
| 4.00 p.m. | Came under direct laying, seemingly from three hostile batteries while crossing ridge S. of Fontaine. These guns secured direct hits on "Harlequin" and "Hydra", we only escaping by steering a zig-zag course. |
| 4.5 p.m. | Spotted one battery near Church at F.21.d.8.2. and silenced it. |
| 4.10 p.m. | Spotted second battery at about L.21.d.2.4. and silenced it. The third battery was also silenced as it troubled us no more. |
| 4.15 p.m. | While proceeding along S. side of village spotted two machine-gun emplacements about 400 x south-west of Church and secured direct hits. |
| 4.20 p.m. | Reached west corner of village, turned about and came back again to the east corner, getting into touch there with "Hadrian" and "Hong Kong". |
| 4.45 p.m. | Saw infantry re-enter village without opposition. |
| 4.55 p.m. | Visibility too low for further shooting, also supplies of petrol and ammunition running out. |
| 5.00 p.m. | Got out of Osprey and together with O.C. 7 Sect. and O.C. "Hadrian" and "Hong Kong" verified map location F.22.a.9.9. and best route home. |
| 5.10 p.m. | Proceeded south-west, striking the Fontaine-Notre-Dame-Cantaing road about F.22.c.1, thence to Cantaing. |
| 7.10 p.m. | Autovac trouble in Cantaing. |
| 8.45 p.m. | Repaired autovac and proceeded by road towards La Justice. |
| 9.20 p.m. | Engine overheated, so stopped to cool. |
| 9.45 p.m. | Re-started engine and proceeded. |
| 10.15 p.m. | Reached rallying point at Orival Wood. |

### GENERAL NOTES.

*Lewis Guns.* These were constantly jamming owing to the heat of the Osprey and the fact that the deflector bags would not take up the empties quick enough.

*Engine Oil.* This oil (Mobiloil) was too thin for the work and caused overheating.

*Reflectors.*   It was impossible to use these owing to the fascine which obscured the view, and also because of the faulty surface which gave a poor and distorted image.

*Morale.*   I have nothing but praise for all members of the the crew, who stuck to their posts under most trying conditions without a waver. My driver— 91500 Gnr. Main—drove for 18 hours in all: 7 hours continuously on 20/xi/17 and 11 hours continuously on 21/xi/17.

I have the honour to be, Sir,
Your obedient servant,
K. E. HUGHES, 2nd-Lt.

12.45 p.m.                     O.C. "Havoc",
25/xi/17.                      7 Sect. 23 Coy.
H Bn., Tank Corps.

From: O.C. Tank "Hermosa",
    No. 7 Sect., 23 Coy., H Battn.
To: O.C. No. 7 Sect., 23 Coy., H Battn.
    Tank Corps.

Ref. Marcoing 1:10,000.
Sir,
    With reference to actions on 20th and 21st Nov. 1917, I have the honour to report as follows:

6.10 a.m.   (Zero—10 mins.) "Hermosa" (No. 1 Main Body) left starting point immediately in rear of "Hadrian".
6.55 a.m.   Crossed own support line 100 x east of Argyle Road.
7.20 a.m.   Crossed own front line, infantry following 70 x in rear.
7.29 a.m.   Crossed Plush Trench.
7.38 a.m.   Crossed Valley Trench by means of fascine already laid.
8.12 a.m.   Crossed Valley Support Trench by means of fascine already laid.
9.55 a.m.   Received message "Assume battle formation", from "Hadrian".
10.8 a.m.   Opened fire on enemy who had been compelled to leave farmhouse (L.21.d.45.85) by fire from "Havoc" and "Hadrian" (Ref.: Niergnies 1.20,000).

10.55 a.m.   Received disc message from "Hadrian": "Return to rallying point."

1.5 p.m.   Reached rallying point.

21st Nov. 1917. Ref. Niergnies 1 : 20,000.

10.30 a.m.   Received orders to proceed to Beetroot Factory (L.13.c.5.8.).

1.5 p.m.   Reached above location and received orders from O.C. 23 Coy. to attack Fontaine-Notre-Dame.

1.25 p.m.   Left factory and proceeded in line 200 x interval between Ospreys.

2.55 p.m.   Came across infantry and was informed that they were being held up by intense machine-gun fire from Cantaing Mill. I proceeded to this place and was in time to get my guns to bear on enemy, who were retiring. On way to my objective the infantry were being constantly held up by machine-guns which were placed in the open. I succeeded in locating one, which was put out of action by one of my guns. 800 x from Fontaine I changed into fourth speed and quickly made for the village.

4.3 p.m.   Reached village and entered by rough track on south-west side. Stopped Osprey and opened fire on what appeared to be a gun emplacement dug in on left side of street west of church. With the exception of about a dozen of the enemy, whom we fired at, the village appeared deserted. Most of the streets on the west side were traversed until I reached the main street. At this point I turned to the right and proceeded along main street until clear of the village on the Fontaine-Cambrai road. Enemy were seen retiring but I did not open fire as they were some distance away and the light was very bad. I then turned about and came back by the same street until I reached the station street, along which I proceeded some little distance. The light was by this time very bad, and as I had not seen any of our troops I decided to return to rallying point. Coming back through the village I saw a light in house and, together with one man, entered and found that it was only inhabited by French civilians. (Report torn here)—met few of

Argyle and Sutherland Highlanders who had
entered village. I waited until the infantry had
5.50 p.m.   consolidated and left at 5.50 p.m.
10.00 p.m.  Reached rallying point.

NOTES.

1. Left front gun was hit by shell when in front of village and one man was slightly wounded. This gun was completely put out of action and could not be replaced, having jammed in turret.
2. The officer's gun in front had gas regulator key shot away by machine-gun fire and was rendered useless as a machine-gun, but could be used for firing single shots.
3. One gun fired well, but the remainder behaved very badly, giving many No. 2 and No. 3 stoppages.
4. Osprey stopped twice on return journey owing to inferior petrol.
5. Engine got very hot owing to engine oil, which was too thin for the work.

I have the honour to be, Sir,
Your obedient servant,
S. GEORGE KEAY, Lieut.
O.C. "Hermosa", 23 Company,
H. Battn., Tank Corps,
11 a.m.                                24th November 1917


To: O.C. 23 Coy., H Battn.,
    Tank Corps.
        January 6th, 1918.

With reference to inquiry of 3/1/18, I have the honour to submit the following:

During the recent actions No. 7 Section, 23 Company, was engaged in the fighting in or around four villages:

On the 20th, Ribécourt and Marcoing.

On the 21st, Cantaing and Fontaine.

This section together with one other tank captured the village of Fontaine on the 21st.

Numerous prisoners were taken on the 20th and handed to infantry after a battery of machine-guns had been destroyed near Marcoing.

On the 21st a trench mortar battery and three field-guns were silenced in the neighbourhood of Cantaing Mill and Fontaine respectively.

The three tanks of this Section rallied after each action

without injury to tanks, or casualty amongst personnel, after having been in action for eight hours on the 20th and eleven hours on the 21st.

This, I think, constitutes a record of work accomplished by a section without loss of life or material.

D. E. HICKEY, Capt.
O.C. No. 7 Section,
23 Coy.

January 6th, 1918.

## G.H.Q. OFFICIAL COMMUNIQUÉ

Thursday morning.

Yesterday evening our troops, moving forward north of Cantaing, attacked and captured the village of Fontaine-Notre Dame (two miles from the western outskirts of Cambrai), together with a number of prisoners.

Thursday night.

On the southern battle front the day has been spent in consolidating the large area over which our troops have advanced during the last two days. This has been successfully carried out, except at Fontaine-Notre-Dame, which the enemy has retaken by a counter-attack.

Much credit is due to the transportation services for the rapidity with which the concentration for the operations of the last few days was effected. The roads and railways, both broad-gauge and light, have been developed and, since the advance, extended in a manner which has contributed largely to the success of our preparations and subsequent operations.

---

# II. THE MARCH RETREAT
## CAPTAIN HICKEY'S REPORT OF ATTACK ON BUS

To: O.C. "B" Company,
8th Tank Battn.
April 3rd, 1918.
*Map. Ref.: France Sheet 57c. Edition 2.* 1/40,000.

At about 11 a.m. on the 24th March 1918, I received orders from you for the tanks of my Section—Nos. 27, 28 and 29—to go into action at Bus and "demonstrate" in front of the village, so as to enable the infantry at Bertincourt to retire on to a line running through "O", 11, 17, 23, 29 and 35 Central. The tanks to rally after the action at Geuedicourt.

The three tanks of my section reached Villers-au-Flos. Nos. 28 and 29 (Lt. Miles and 2nd-Lt. Beddard) developed mechanical trouble soon after, and were compelled to stop for repairs.

I continued towards Bus with No. 27 (2nd-Lt. Mickle), which went into action about noon.

I was at the Crucifix Corner (O.15.d.40.20) at the commencement of the action; but observing four or five men, who appeared to be in khaki, rush out of the village of Bus with their "hands-up" towards the tanks soon after the demonstration had begun, I set out with 2nd-Lt. Macfarlane to meet two of them, who were approaching the trenches in the neighbourhood of O.21.b.90.90. These two were infantrymen who had been captured by the Germans earlier in the day, and made prisoners at Bus. On the approach of the tanks towards the village the Germans had fled, and they had regained their liberty. They stated that German cavalry had been in the vicinity of Bus, but had left on seeing the tanks.

2nd-Lt. Macfarlane left me here to go and investigate one of his tanks which was out of action.

Having learnt that the village was clear of the enemy from these two men, and seeing that the enemy artillery was becoming active, I went out towards Bus to rally the tanks.

I came across a third man who had escaped and he confirmed the statements of the previous two.

A fourth was shot through the head as I approached him; hostile machine-guns at this time being fairly active from the vicinity of O.16.

I proceeded on towards Bus, and entered 2nd-Lt. Mickle's tank. The remainder of the tanks by this time had commenced to return.

At the rallying point at Geuedicourt I was instructed by Major Pratt, D.S.O., M.C., to continue to Courcelette.

# III. BATTLE OF AMIENS

## PERSONNEL OF NO. 7 SECTION

*The following personnel of No. 7 Section will be retained to go into action:*

**Section H.Q.**
Captain D. E. Hickey
202016 Gnr. Stittle, E.W.

**Tank "H24"**
2nd-Lt. S. S. Jefferies
202042 Cpl. Dunn, J. E.
110229 Gnr. Black, W. G.
78511 ,, Hopkins, W.
78506 ,, McIntyre, H.
97038 ,, Harris, W. F.
305539 ,, Neal, H. L. (Brown)

**Tank "H25"**
2nd-Lt. H. W. Humphreys
78486 Cpl. Stanton, W. F.
92880 Gnr. Williams, G.
94807 ,, Confrey, W.
305320 ,, Charnock, F.
306258 ,, Wigham, W.

**Tank "H32"**
2nd-Lt. C. E. Few
70188 Sgt. Vicary
97363 Gnr. Armstrong
92738 ,, Newman
305317 ,, Ford
305823 ,, Carter

**Strength:**

|  |  |  |
|---|---|---|
| Officers | 4 | |
| Sergeants | 1 | 6/8/18 |
| Corporals | 2 | |
| Gunners | 14 | |

21 plus 1 replacement.

*The five uninjured after twice in action were:*
Cpl. Stanton, Gnr. Stittle, Gnr. Neal, Gnr. Charnock, Gnr. Wigham.

# CAPTAIN HICKEY'S REPORT OF NIGHT ATTACK

From: O.C. No. 7 Section,
  B Coy.,
    8th Tank Battalion.
To: O.C. B Coy.,
    8th Tank Battalion.

12/8/18.

*Map Ref.:* 1/20,000. 62 D. S.E.

I received orders about 3.30 p.m. on 10th August 1918, as follows:

To join the 37th Battalion A.I.F. with my section of tanks at 8 p.m. on the same day at the Hospital in Q.30.c. on the Warfusee-Abancourt Road and to head the battalion along the road with a view to penetrating the enemy line, presumed to be at La Flaque, to the cross roads in R.28.c., about 1,500 yards from La Flaque. Zero hour to be 9.30 p.m. Thence to proceed northwards along a prescribed route to the high ground west of Chuignolles. The tanks to move one on either side of the road and one on the road. Close touch to be kept between each other and the infantry.

·    ·    ·    ·    ·

I reported to the Commanding Officer of the 37th Battalion A.I.F., at 8 p.m. near the Hospital, and received instructions to bring the tanks into position at the head of the infantry at 9.15 p.m. Zero hour had been altered to 10 p.m.

At 9.15 p.m. the tanks in the following order: H24, H25 and H32, moved forward at the head of the battalion, which was following immediately behind in file. It was quite dark at 10 p.m. The three tanks were kept on the road as, after consultation with the Commanding Offcer of the 37th Battalion, it was agreed that it would be very dangerous for tanks to proceed along the sides of the road without getting "ditched" owing to old earthworks, which would be most treacherous in the dark, and dumps which were likely to impede the advance of the tanks.

An officer guide was appointed from the 37th Battalion A.I.F. to be responsible for direction. I accompanied the C.O. of the 37th Battalion under his instructions during the movement.

Enemy opposition was first encountered about 400 or 500 yards east of La Flaque. The enemy, hearing the noise of the tanks, put up flares which exposed the whole situation quite plainly and the whole column came under very heavy machine-gun fire.

The infantry then got down into the ditches on the south side of the road. The tanks opened heavy fire but could not locate enemy machine-guns and had no effect whatsoever upon the fire of the enemy. The infantry continued along the ditch in short advances and then, suffering severe casualties, hesitated. A runner reported the tanks to be returning. The C.O. conferred with me and said the tanks were to continue the advance. I immediately rushed forward along the road and met the tanks returning. I ordered them to turn about and continue the advance. At the same time, whilst the C.O. was urging the infantry forward, he was killed.

As the tanks were preparing to advance again, I met the Adjutant of the 37th Battalion A.I.F., who told me that the infantry were retiring in extended order. I informed him that the tanks were going forward to continue the attack; but, the infantry now being disorganized, he said it would be impossible for them to follow, and so I ordered the tanks to retire.

After the tanks had retired about 150 yards I met the C.O. of the battalion following the 37th Battalion, who instructed me to stop the tanks and await orders.

Instructions were eventually received to cover the retirement of the infantry, and when they were in position the tanks themselves to retire.

This movement was completed by 3.45 a.m.

D. E. HICKEY, Capt.
O.C. No. 7 Section,
B Coy., 8th Tank Battalion.

9.50 a.m.
12th August 1918.
In the Field.

9 781847 347268